The Witness
of Combines

KENT MEYERS

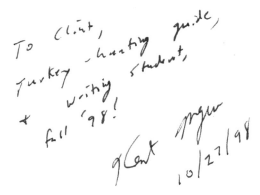

To Clint,
turkey-hunting guide,
& writing student,
fall '98!

Kent Myers
10/27/98

University of Minnesota Press
Minneapolis / London

Published by the University of Minnesota Press
111 Third Avenue South, Suite 290
Minneapolis, MN 55401-2520
http://www.upress.umn.edu

Library of Congress Cataloging-in-Publication Data

Meyers, Kent.
    The witness of combines / Kent Meyers.
        p.   cm.
    ISBN 0-8166-3105-0 (pb : alk. paper)
    1. Meyers, Kent. 2. Morgan Region (Minn.)—Biography.
3. Morgan Region (Minn.)—Social life and customs.
4. Country life—Minnesota—Morgan Region. I. Title.
F614.M75M49   1998
977.6'35—dc21   98-12898
                                                          CIP

Printed in the United States of America on acid-free paper

The University of Minnesota is an equal-opportunity educator
and employer.

10 09 08 07 06 05 04 03 02 01 00 99 98   10 9 8 7 6 5 4 3 2 1

The Witness of Combines

To my parents
Wayne and Marguerite Meyers

CONTENTS

PREFACE

The essays in this collection were written over several years, as my awareness of what it meant to love a place and lose it grew and changed. As a child I identified with the small farm on which I was raised. I felt myself a part of the land, and all of the important formative experiences of my life occurred upon and in relationship to it, as well as in relationship to my family, and the small community where I lived.

My father died when I was sixteen, and with his death the farm passed out of our family's hands. These essays explore the meaning of that double loss. In doing so, they explore the richness of family life, the nature of work, and the ways that communities can both reify and redeem loss.

Three people deserve first thanks for the formation of this book: my father, Wayne; my mother, Marguerite; and my wife, Zindie.

My father taught me to work, to persevere, and to look upon the world with equanimity and respect—all essential qualities for me as a writer and a human being.

My mother—though she no doubt has forgotten it—once told me: "You have to use your talents." I've been trying ever since to do so. Luckily my mother managed to pass along some of her amazing sense of humor, which sustained me when the use of talents seemed a little crazy.

Zindie had no idea what she was getting into when she married me. At the time I had no symptoms of getting up in the early morning to lock myself away for several hours to write. Writing is a kind of intense privacy. Zindie has allowed it, somehow, to become part of our relationship, and that has deepened and strengthened my writing.

The community of Morgan, Minnesota, shaped me and, when I most needed it, existed *as* community for me. Many individuals there were true neighbors.

The prairieland of southern Minnesota, and all the creatures that reside there, were patient in forming me, and the spirit of the Minnesota River, the ancient, great River Warren, still lives within my heart.

My brothers and sisters taught me how to live—how to get along but also how to stand up for myself. If I haven't named each of them in these essays, they deserve to be named here, from oldest to youngest, as we memorized the list as children: Kevin, Renee, Joel, Colin, Ann, Cyndee, Marie, Paul. (I fit between Renee and Joel.)

All my teachers deserve thanks, but especially two professors at the University of Minnesota, Morris: Don Spring, whose love of language and understanding of how it works astonished me when I entered his "Technique and Form in Poetry" class, surely the most formative class I've ever taken; and Nathaniel Hart, who had the courage, grace, and insight to suggest I might actually be able to write this very book. He read one essay and told me there were more. It took me twenty years to realize what he saw—but real teachers, thank God, are patient, and will wait a long time to discover their influence.

Stewart Bellman has given me constant support, friendship, and advice, and has served as reader for many of these essays. I have valued his encouragement and insights, and have learned much, about both writing and life, from him.

Dick Hicks has deepened my understanding of light, color, form, and shape, through the ongoing discussions we have about art. In doing so, he has deepened my understanding of the world and increased my capacity to write about it.

Linda Raga read many of these essays when she was a student of mine, but rather than merely read them, as most students would, she commented on them with insight and understanding.

Al Masarik has shared the writing life and let me laugh about it.

Temma Ehrenfeld has given me guidance, advice, and support.

Todd Orjala recognized the potential in an initially unworthy manuscript and insisted upon that potential. He has been a true editor who saw the overall shape of the book and brought it out of me.

Linda Lincoln's careful copyediting clarified the book and prevented various stylistic gaffes from being made public.

Several of these essays were published in magazines or literary journals, in slightly different form, over the past several years. "The Witness of Combines" and "Birds Against the Glass" were published in *Notre*

Dame Magazine, under the titles, respectively, "One Final Harvest" and "The Rightness of Birds." "A Constellation of Cockleburs" was published in the *Georgia Review,* "Straightening the Hammermill" in *Many Mountains Moving,* "Old Waters" in the *North Dakota Quarterly* (under the title "Prairieland"), "Windbreak" and "Going Back" in the *Minnesota Monthly* (under the title "Straight Lines and Long Winds"), and "Rocks, Roots, and Weeds" in the *Lake Street Review.* I thank the editors and staff of all these publications, but especially Stan Lindberg at the *Georgia Review* and Kerry Temple at *Notre Dame Magazine,* who have been supportive far beyond the call of editorship.

Finally, I have to thank Tom Herbeck and Wendy Mendoza. Through their friendship and criticism, and the wonderful examples of their own writing, they formed me as a writer and a thinker. Tom taught me to experiment, to never merely accept what is given, to look for new ways to say things and to leave things unsaid, to always seek new forms, the endless possibilities. Wendy taught me how images really work, their mystery and power, and what the names of things really are. She read every one of these essays, has been a guiding force in the shaping of this book, and has never let me get away with cheap words, dishonest images, or phrases that escape the center.

The Witness
of Combines

I don't remember being told that the combines were coming, but I knew they would, so when they arrived they went to work as if I had planned them. So much of my life that summer and fall exists to me now as a kind of habit-molded dream. I can't distinguish between making decisions about work and life and being decided by work and life. It wasn't until three years later, when for a composition class in college I wrote an essay about my father's death, that I wept for that death. It's not that I was holding myself aloof from grief. It was more that life for me, strangely, continued much as it had before. A week after my father's death I participated in a regional high school speaking contest, and I remember the sympathy in my English teacher's face when she met me in the hall. The tears moistening her eyes seemed odd and out of place to me. There was work to do.

We rose every morning and put on our work clothes and went out to the expectant cattle and began to fill baskets with ground corn and carry them down the rows of bunks, and the cattle knew nothing and cared nothing. Sweat formed, and muscles loosened. This was the way it had been for us as long as we could remember, this work in the mornings and afternoons, unchanged by any absence. There was something natural and right in that unalteration, and the sweat that returned, easy and full of the body's grace, to the surface of the skin.

The work went on, through the sorting and selling of the cattle, and the preparation of the soil and its planting, all unavoidable and never thought to be avoided—and all that time the combines were coming. The neighbors were wondering whether Wayne Meyers's sons were going to manage all right, eyeing the crops we'd planted with critical, professional eyes and, seeing that the crops were good, maintaining their silence, keeping the important illusion that we and they both were independent farmers doing work defined by the fences.

Only in their own talk—which I imagine now taking place at the grain elevator and the pool hall, and over those sagging fences buried in long grass where two tractors stop and neighbors converse for a while— did an action begin to form. The talk urged something into existence as we went about our daily work that spring and summer, and the crops rose, and pollen floated, and the air swelled with the milky smell of ripening corn. The unripe future ripened, and words touched against it tenderly, to test the moment. When the moment came, corn and community ripe at the same time, there appeared in our driveway combines and trucks, coming down the long, gradual slope from the county road, raising dust. I watched them knowing they would come but not expecting them, and I pointed them to the fields as if with my own voice I had called them, with my own finger beckoned.

The voice not asking for help was the same as the voices that shaped that help unasked for. We could have harvested the corn ourselves, though it would have been difficult with school in session. We could have hired the work done. But harvest is everything on the plains, the summation of all effort, the gauge of all knowledge and judgment, and the combines came as a communal action, out of respect for my father, an acknowledgment of his passing, and a healing gesture from the human, communal heart.

It took two days. Had we done it ourselves it would have taken two weeks. The neighbors with their combines glided up and down the fields, dumping the corn from their tanks into trucks that we drove directly to the elevator, selling it instead of storing it for feed, since we knew this was the last year we'd farm, the old patterns broken, the cattle's steamy breath not to fill the barns this coming winter, their hooves not to tramp the frozen ground as they waited to be fed.

The neighbors let us do what we could, in all the dignity of accomplishment, the quiet of singular achievement, and never was advice offered by any of the men who drove the roads, who slowed to watch our progress that summer, and kept to themselves our transgressions, until the time ripened when we might by their help be more dignified, might stand within our harvest as adults and men, and they witnesses to who we were, not mere helpers—witnesses formed by history and community, stamped by the land, this harvest a testament to our father's guidance and his sons' abilities and learning, the shelled corn pouring from the spouts and brimming in the trucks, lapping against the sideboards like labor liquid and refined.

Later the talk came back to us, through the crooked meanderings of rumor—rectitude and dignity casting the words to the winds so they were carried through the community before reaching us—that the men who ran the combines spoke to each other of how they couldn't believe we had grown corn this productive, had brought from the land—not so much out of knowledge of the land, but from our knowledge of our father's knowledge, doing what we knew he would have done—this harvest that, the rumors finally told us, surpassed that of many of the men who combined for us.

For two days the combines roamed up and down the rows, and trucks ran regular circuits between our farm and the elevator in town, and my mother spent all day cooking for men who, many of them, had never set foot in our house and never would again, not because they weren't welcome but because they were neighbors—not relatives, who are allowed in regardless of affection, and not friends, who enter for the ease of being there—but neighbors, for whom necessity rules. Through the door of necessity they walked into our lives, though they had always been there, silent and observant and for the most part ignored, just as we had been in theirs.

Then the fields lay bare. The harvest finished, the neighbors dispersed to their own fields while we continued in ours, discing the cornstalks and then plowing, preparing the land for whoever would rent it come spring. Once again the land appeared to be farmed by individual farmers making their own uses of it.

The alluvial soil on which I grew, one of the richest in the world, a Clarion-Webster silt-clay-loam, is formed from glacial winds and old waters and centuries of wetland grasses. Busted by German and Scandinavian settlers, the sod turned pitch black when the long grasses decomposed. Corn and soybean crops today grow from a reservoir of millions of plants that have fallen—prairie coneflower and swamp milkweed and phlox and false indigo and blazing star and purple loosestrife and bluestem grass and Indian grass and grama grass.

The soil itself of a virgin, long-grass prairie is nearly barren. All the nutrients are drawn into the blaze of flower and stem, flowing constantly through the plants, and things so interdependent and intertwined that nearly every molecule of nutrient is taken in by the tangled root system that hardens the soil and is itself merely the substrate of exchange. Only since the sod was turned, barely one hundred years ago, have we been able to speak of the "richness" of the soil itself, the nutrients now, even when the land is so green in the summer it stuns the eye, lying mostly within the soil, monoculture farming being unable to draw them all up, so that farmers spread fertilizers to encourage single crops and douse with chemicals the weeds—and a weed is merely a plant that has lost its relationship to other plants—that attempt to use the remaining nutrients.

Still, the virgin prairie's way of being emerges in the communities that have shaped themselves upon it, though the tangled words that form these communities are dumb to what they form, like the roots of plants that cannot know the blossom. The combines came, dumb to everything but necessity, ignorant of any knowledge but that of time and winter. The talk that brought them was not about relationships and ritual or the fulfillment of patterns or how an individual becomes a person by being drawn into and dignified by the mutual weave of community life. These things have been left for me to say.

Communities on the northern plains are made manifest by disaster. Thus it is that an individual or family can be graced by loss, as the land, never stopping or waiting, absorbs the seasons, and the people who have chosen to live upon it must make the ritual responses. When these responses cannot be made, the community—which appears to be only a collection of individuals working their own land—shapes itself by its talk, and is made manifest in the clumsy, lumbering grace of combines silhouetted against the far sky, and the small dust they raise on the road, blown instantly away, and by the unnameable faces of neighbors made indistinct by the refraction of memory and who don't need to be remembered or thanked beyond the restrained and ordinary thanks that comes when a job is finished and that is offered like water is offered, with the knowledge that we all thirst.

In the moment of disaster for one of their members, these prairie communities draw into themselves, out of their rich substrate of tradition, out of the deepest sources of their culture, all the quiet charities and powerful stories that have told them how to live—stories that have never, in ordinary times, prevented them from bickering and gossiping, and coveting their neighbor's machinery. But when the worst that can happen happens, when the resources of the individual or family are exhausted, talk, like the tendrils of roots, draws from the old stories their essential meaning and power, and land and stories and people and belief for a time become one, and though no one expects help, everyone knows it will come.

I suspect that some of the men who drove down our driveway and into our fields that summer were men with whom my father had had disagreements. I know that many of them were fundamentally different from him in their beliefs and outlooks, as different as lead plant from coneflower. Yet when he died, these men appeared to witness his sons.

I will take them. I will take their silence that summer, the respect they showed us by letting us succeed on our own. I will take them in all their restraint and imperfection. They knew what was necessary. They were neighbors. When necessity called they drew up into their individual differences the strengths of their traditions and formed of those strengths a community and a culture, and made us part of a whole.

I will take their witness. I will take a man who will not take thanks, a man whose face I can't even remember and who has no need to be remembered, hidden behind the reflection off Plexiglas or the dust raised by the immense machine he has driven slow miles over gravel roads to help me, to help my family—because the corn is ripe, the time is ripe, the talk is ripe. I will take men I might not even like, and I will take their compliments directed away from me, and their faith that nevertheless I would come to hear them.

I will take their witness to my passage into the community of human beings, and the community of the land itself, the ancient waters and plants whispering in it, the cycles that repeat, that end but are never ended, the stories that go so far back and are so rich they begin with the beginning, the stories of our needs, of our communion with all things and each other, of our living and dying and being.

Windbreak

My older brother, Kevin, built the windbreak as a Future Farmers of America farm improvement project. It was a seven-foot-tall wall of boards, extending from one corner of the west barn south about forty yards along the grove. An old grove loses its power against wind, lofts its crown too high in the air, and the wind rams through the loose picket of trunks. To anyone choosing to settle on the prairie rather than roam over it, stopping wind is a noble enterprise. In O. E. Rölvaag's *Giants in the Earth,* one of Per Hansa's many victories over the prairie is planting saplings from the Sioux River to surround his dwelling.

Modern groves are scientifically designed, in layers, rising from bush to shrub to small tree to large. Growing a new grove, however, is a years-long affair. A wall of boards to protect cattle takes only a few weeks to build, and does the job less aesthetically but as well.

In fact it does the job better. Kevin used tongue-in-groove boards, which seal out wind as effectively as glass. He made a perfect windbreak. If he had left gaps between the boards—if he had been willing to slow the wind down rather than break it—Kevin could have saved us a lot of hard work. In the heat of summer he had forgotten that wind in the winter carries a burden of snow, and that when the wind stops, it drops that burden on top of whatever has stopped it.

There was nothing between his windbreak and the Black Hills, nothing for five hundred miles—all of South Dakota and half of Minnesota, the wind picking up snow from the draws and gullies of western South Dakota, from the Missouri River valley, from the level plains of eastern South Dakota, rangeland and farmland, grass and hay and cornstalks, and flat, black plowland—howling into Minnesota with its load, whistling and hooting, freight-laden and full.

Then it hit that windbreak.

And dropped its snow like lead.

Five hundred miles of snow piled up around Kevin's windbreak. He received the FFA farm improvement award that year, but he should have left gaps between the boards, should have let part of the wind through so the drift would form ten feet east of the windbreak. Without gaps, the snow covered the windbreak and got so crusted over and hard that the cattle walked right over it, out of the feedlot and into the grove. From there they could go anywhere.

So, many times every winter, we dug snow trenches into the drift on the leeward side of the windbreak. The morning after a night of wind, when our regular chores were done, the cattle fed and content, Dad gathered us together (Kevin, me, Joel, and Colin), found a shovel for each of us, and we trudged to the windbreak and started to dig.

Every time, Dad would pause at some point and lean on his shovel. We all took that as a signal to do likewise. As we gazed at the cattle, Dad observed, mildly, that there should have been gaps between the boards. Then he returned to work, and we reluctantly did the same, until we had dug a six-foot-deep trench extending the length of the windbreak. If we were lucky, there wasn't another big wind for several days and the trench lasted long enough to make our work seem worthwhile, the cattle climbing up the crusted snow to stare dumbly out of white faces at the angular gap where flowing snow should have been.

The trench, though, always filled in again—sometimes overnight, sometimes a month later—and we always dug it out again, repeating what was to us a wearisome and monotonous task. We appreciated the windbreak for its kindness to the cattle, but we grew frustrated, seeing the wind as insistent on ruining our labors. Dad's voice, however, as he leaned on his shovel and gazed at the cattle, was always mild, merely making an observation: gaps between the boards would have saved us all this work. He didn't seem to mind the work, didn't seem bothered by it.

On the prairie, only wind is permanent. We were frustrating wind; it wasn't frustrating us. I think Dad realized the difference early in his life. In his early twenties he took over the family farm from his father, who, through alcoholism and poor decisions, had accumulated bad debts. Dad dropped out of school in eighth grade, influenced by his mother, who thought it was time he worked seriously. Education, however, meant much to him, and when he was eighteen, he went back to school, picking up where he'd left off. My mother, six years younger, was going to school at the same time and she claims he was quite the phenomenon, especially among the girls—this older, quiet, handsome man among teenagers, steadfastly acquiring an education, unconcerned with what people might think or with the oddness of his position.

He was tired of the farm, tired of how his own father had never gotten ahead. When he graduated from high school at the age of twenty-two, he went to business college, intending to gain a degree and make something of his life. After one year, however, when he returned to the farm for the summer with his newly acquired knowledge of bookkeeping and money, he discovered just how poorly his father was running things, how desperate the financial straits of his parents were.

He was the youngest son, the last chance for saving the farm. His older brothers had all gone on to other things, and his sisters had no desire—and at that time, no means or conventions—by which they could take over the land. So he stayed, and when the new school term began, he wasn't there among the desks. He was harvesting a corn crop planted by his father.

My mother, meanwhile, was back from World War II. She had been an Army nurse, a lieutenant, in a hospital in France until she contracted tuberculosis. For two years she lay in a bed in a sanitorium in Minneapolis, containing the disease, until she gained enough health to leave, with one lung virtually ruined. In the prime of my health and strength as a teenager, I once laughed at her when she quickly grew out of breath chasing some chickens that had gone into the garden. Quietly, without accusation, she told me she only had one good lung. I'd known of the disease, but not of the invisible loss she had suffered, and my laughter, because of the quiet way she told me, turned not to shame but to respect.

My mother and father were reacquainted when she returned to her family after the sanitorium. Under the terms of her disability discharge, she could further her education, but for the Army to defray the cost, it had to be advanced study in the field in which she had already started. So, although she had a nursing degree and realized later in life that she would have preferred to teach, she returned to school in Minneapolis to gain a bachelor's degree in nursing.

My father at the time was deeply in love with a devout Catholic woman—too devout in fact for marriage; she decided to become a nun. I have never been sure how this fit into his decision to return to the farm, but it must have been a blow, for they were close and he had hopes of a future with her. How strange, I've always thought, to lose a lover to a rival you cannot blame or hate, a rival that embodies the values you yourself aspire to, to watch your lover, too good, recede into her goodness, her idealism and spirituality— the very things you love in her carrying her away.

Gradually my father pulled his father's farm out of debt. He worked constantly and managed meticulously. His mother, made pinched by years of deprivation and able to control her son with authority she couldn't exercise on her husband, decided that room and board were enough pay for what he did and that he didn't need money for excesses like recreation. The town of Morgan, Minnesota, had a movie theater at that time, and he managed to see a movie once a week, his sole form of relaxation.

He'd known my mother in high school, though he had been a young man then, she a girl, with no thought of attraction between them. Now, however, they met again, both adults, both with their own forms of hardship and experience, both back, by different routes, to the place where they had started. A relationship grew, between my mother's trips to Minneapolis for classes and my father's constant work, and in time they knew they'd marry.

My father's mother didn't approve. She told him, thinking it was a secret, that the woman he was serious about had had tuberculosis, and would never endure the hardships of farm life. I don't think my grandmother was merely vicious. The comment speaks volumes about her sense of her own life's hardships. However, the tuberculosis was no secret to my father, my mother having told him long before. When he told her of his mother's words, she said: "But Wayne, we've been through all this already."

"I know," he said, "but you have to know what she's saying."

Early in their relationship he revealed his own secret, that his father was an alcoholic. "Wayne!" my mother tells me she exclaimed, "I've known that for *years!*" It was common knowledge in the community. I sense, in the fact that he felt it was a secret he had to tell her and in her reaction, a great deal of unnecessary shame. My mother liked her father-in-law. He was quiet, soft-spoken, unassuming, but grappling with a demon he couldn't control.

His son, however, had seen the effects of the demon and was determined not to be caught by it. For several years after he married, he would return from trips to town with a six-pack of beer and drink a beer a day until it was gone. But one day he said, "If I keep this up, I'll end up like my father," and that was the end of alcohol in his house. He kept a bottle of *Four Roses* whiskey in the cabinet above the kitchen sink for guests who wanted to mix a drink, and every few years he'd go to the liquor store in town for a new bottle. He drank a beer at family reunions, but other than that, he never touched alcohol, never went to the bar or the pool hall. His entire social life was focused around his family.

He quit smoking with the same kind of will and directness with which he gave up alcohol. He was a two-pack-a-day smoker, but when he realized the dangers to his health, he simply decided to stop—and stopped. There was no fanfare, no imposed stress on the family, no relapse. If offered a cigarette by a smoker, he accepted and enjoyed it, but he never allowed it to drag him back into the habit. Having seen the struggles of other people trying to quit smoking, I find this fact amazing, yet it also seems utterly consistent with someone who at eighteen would return to ninth grade, independent, indifferent to social expectations, knowing his own mind.

His father died in 1948 and he married in 1950.

When he married, his mother deeded him a hundred acres, half the farm. On this he supported his new wife and growing family, continuing to work the other hundred acres on a rental basis from his mother, who moved to Franklin, Minnesota. He paid off all his father's debts and brought the farm back from bankruptcy, even going so far as to seek out people to whom his father owed money. When this news got out, he had no trouble finding creditors, who came to him with long-forgotten bills. He paid them all, impoverishing himself but gaining a reputation as the most honest man in the community.

In 1958 his mother died without a will. The hundred acres that belonged to her were equally divided among her seven children. Most of them, realizing that Dad had essentially paid for the land by paying off its debts, were in favor of selling their portions to him at below-market prices. Dissensions arose, however, and in the end Dad bought the farm at market prices from his brothers and sisters. He was never bitter over this—and in truth it's hard to know where justice lay, what an inheritance is worth—but he always felt that he had paid twice for the farm.

It made him cautious. Having spent so much of his sweat and money salvaging this one farm, he grew wary of buying more land. He stayed with the two hundred acres he had and managed to raise nine children on it, keeping them for the most part oblivious to their poverty. By raising livestock he was able to increase the profits from the crops, but also his workload and his day-to-day involvement. Crops can be left to grow; livestock needs constant tending. He never went

anywhere, never took vacations. He was thoroughly a
farmer.

There is pleasant irony in much of this—that a man
determined to leave the farm should become so closely
identified with it that I, his son, cannot think of him
without thinking of the land, of him upon it, watching
it, walking over it, the land part of his character, and
he—in the way he worked it and brought forth its
yield—part of its nature. He and the land are not syn-
onymous, but neither are they separate, distinct enti-
ties. He formed the place. The place formed him. They
were part of each other.

I can picture him in many ways: dressed in a short-
sleeved shirt, sitting in a lawn chair at a lake on one of
our infrequent Sunday excursions; in a gray suit and tie,
wearing a felt dress hat with a small feather in its band,
going to church on Sunday mornings; talking politics
quietly with one of his brothers or brothers-in-law, in
the living room, on a Saturday night when company
came (and company was always family). But the truest
image I have of him, the one that claims him, speaks
him, addresses who he is, is of him dressed in a long-
sleeved, faded blue chambray shirt and blue jeans,
wearing a straw hat to protect his balding head from
the May sun, sitting on the old International "H" tractor, his pale blue eyes fixed on the front wheel as he
runs it down the furrow left by the corn-planter mark-
er, planting the straightest corn rows in the county,
rows that would run up the field with the precision of
railroad tracks.

It is the frailty suggested by this image, and the determination within that frailty, and the association with

the land, the way that he and the land were engaged in a common, difficult enterprise, that speaks his being. He always wore long sleeves when working, no matter how hot the day or how difficult the work, and he always wore that straw hat, recognizing how easily the sun could harm him and how much he needed to be out in it. Cabs on tractors were not common then, and when they became common, he couldn't afford one, and so made do with straw hats and long sleeves.

Yet there is tenacity in those eyes, stubbornness, determination. He planted straight corn rows not because they increased his yield or because anyone else cared, but because *he* liked them, because he *liked* them, liked the look of the land in straight rows, because it was his farm, because it expressed him. Those rows were a product not of necessity but of will, desire, and quiet passion.

Life, of course, contains unpleasant as well as pleasant ironies. At the age of fifty-five he finally paid for the land outright, the father now of nine children, five boys and four girls, the oldest nineteen, the youngest five, and he began to think of finally expanding, of buying more land and larger machinery. At last he had found financial breathing room. With more land he could increase his wealth and ultimately decrease his work, and prepare for his oldest son's graduation from college. Kevin had never wanted to do anything but farm, had been climbing on tractors since he was three, and now Dad could ease his son's way into it, expand, set Kevin up, share machinery, and reap some rewards from a lifetime of work.

But at the age of fifty-six he died. On a Palm Sunday afternoon—so unusual to be working on a Sunday—he and I were building up the shares on a spring-tooth harrow, welding hot beads of metal up and down the shares, replacing what had been worn off the previous year by the steel-devouring soil. Then Dad handed me the welding wand, the first time he'd ever done that.

He'd bought a welder early, before most farmers had them, and had taken a class at the high school to learn to use it, but for the most part he had taught himself. Though he saved a great deal of money on repair bills, he never quite perfected welding, tending to keep the welder turned too low for fear of burning through the metal.

When I took a welding class in high school shop, it was something I took to naturally and easily, and did well. When Dad handed me the welding wand that Sunday afternoon, I took it as a sign that he recognized I had surpassed him in a skill important to his livelihood. I accepted the wand with pride, flipped the helmet down, and set to work, running beads of hot metal up and down the shares, loving the way they solidified like ridged fossils.

I had in fact surpassed him at the skill and deserved my sense of pride—any son's sense of pride—in doing something better than my father. Yet he had handed me the wand because he had suffered a small stroke and had grown weak, disoriented, incoherent. My mother found him wandering around the yard, lost, unspeaking, and—her training as a nurse both vital and useless—she recognized the symptoms and took him to the hospital. Three weeks later, having suffered a more massive stroke, he died, on April 13, 1972. I was sixteen.

Like detectives sifting evidence, we put it together later: my mother's sense that something was wrong that Sunday morning finally becoming clear, her feeling that he was slow, distracted; my own sense, beyond even my normal critical and superior teenage knowing, that his welding was spotty; perhaps even the oddity, so out of character and belief, that he was doing unnecessary work on a Sunday.

He died at a season of the year when we had no choice but to continue farming. It was April. Corn needed planting in May. There was no time to find a renter. Kevin, finishing his sophomore year of college, was certainly the most knowledgeable in what had to be done, but Mom wouldn't have him quit school. On weekends he came back from South Dakota State University and worked, but otherwise it was left to me and my two younger brothers, Joel and Colin, to prepare the soil, plant the crops, and continue feeding the cattle before and after school. Land won't wait for grief. We joined together to do what we had to do.

We raised amazing crops, some of the best the farm had ever produced, the weather cooperating completely, and in another strange irony corn, soybean, and cattle prices were all good that year, prompting my mother to comment that it would have pulled Dad completely above water and put him ahead financially.

The next year we rented the land out to a neighbor. It's strange, the mirrors life creates. Dad had tried to

escape the farm through education but had been drawn
back, to find a life in land and family. Once he died,
Mom didn't want her sons trying to farm and go to
school at the same time, and unlike her mother-in-law
she regarded school as essential. She didn't want Kevin
to drop out of college, no doubt never to return, for an
uncertain future, and he wasn't willing to do that either. Had Dad lived for just a few more years he could
have passed the land he'd worked so hard to keep down
to a son. He did so much right, except live long
enough, and perhaps too carefully.

We made decisions. Machinery, like any other large
investment, can't sit around and depreciate without
being used. We decided to hold an auction but retain
the land. Then, when Kevin graduated from college he
found an opportunity to go into ranching in South
Dakota with his future father-in-law. Meanwhile, land
prices rose, and farming got ever bigger, making it difficult for anyone to survive on a mere two hundred acres,
and also more difficult for someone without support to
buy more land.

It became less and less likely that anyone within the
family would be able to swing the huge financial burden a new start in modern farming required. We made
a family decision to sell the land. My mother was feeling isolated out on the farm alone with young children,
especially during the winter, when the wind and snow
could so easily block a road and strand her. She built a
house in town, and the land passed to a neighbor.

I've lived my adult life not owning land, and I've
never quite grown used to it. Given how closely my
father and his land were linked, it's a kind of double

orphanage. Yet, as my father knew, on the prairie, only the shifting wind is permanent. How could he not know it—deep, deep in his heart—given the vicissitudes and difficulties of his life?

Surely that realization was the source of his mildness on those cold winter days, when he leaned on his shovel and watched the curious cattle and remarked how the windbreak should have had gaps between the boards. It is not failure that he worked and sweated for the land and then was unable to keep it for his children. That would be the view of my childhood—that the wind is frustrating us. He knew, as we didn't, that we were frustrating wind, and he knew that though he finally legally owned the land outright, he didn't possess it.

Erazim Kohak, in *The Embers and the Stars,* says: "What I would claim to possess can never belong to me—and whatever belongs to me I can never treat as a possession." My father, through his work upon the land, the love and care he manifested in it, *belonged* to the land, as it finally belonged to him. And he belonged to the wind, that larger wind of which the snow-laden wind of the prairie is sign and symbol, the wind of time and mortality and fate, which propels us all differently. My father's children, though swept along in their lives in different directions, carry part of him, and part of the land that was him, with them. We no longer shovel out windbreaks, but memory remains.

It's a fine thing, I've come to realize, to shovel snow blown from half a continent, while cattle gaze over your shoulder. It's a good thing to know that the five-hundred-mile wind will always return, that the trench—no matter how deeply dug, how straight and square—will be filled in again, will return to its original formlessness.

For a long time I couldn't understand my father's acceptance of a problem so easily solved, his refusal to knock every second board out of the windbreak. It would have taken a few hours, with a good and heavy hammer. I didn't understand how he could state and restate a solution to our problem, and an easy solution at that—and yet, year after year, refuse to implement it.

As I get older, even that is beginning to make sense to me. The nuns in the parochial school I attended taught us that perfection is impossible in this world, though it must be constantly striven for. My father's attitude toward the windbreak teaches a different lesson: perfection is possible in this world, but it can be maintained in small things only, and even that is struggle— but once you achieve perfection, you don't back away from it simply because you discover the magnitude of the work it requires.

My brother defied the nuns and built a perfect windbreak. My father then enlisted hours and hours of our help to struggle against the repercussions of that perfection. He wouldn't knock boards out and ruin it just to save himself some work.

There is much in that attitude that allows the mortal world to impinge upon eternity. My father would have no doubts that, as the five-hundred-mile wind has scattered his children into their individual draws and gullies, so it will also gather them together. He'd have no doubts that the wind, which seems to whirl things into chaos, also straightens them out. He has passed

the barrier that breaks that wind, but it is a barrier designed by a wiser architect than my brother. When, like
snow, we ourselves drop gently out of this wind, I trust
we will find Dad there, no longer needing a shovel,
amid perfect, formless things, mild, and awaiting his
family.

Straightening
the Hammermill

In the winter, in rat-scurrying corncribs, with the dog
waiting and our breath white, we handled the shovels,
dumping corn into the roar of the hammermill while
the Five-Sixty wailed, the rain cap on the top of its muffler opened wide to the sky and blue smoke pouring
out. We couldn't speak over the noise, but we knew
what we were doing, so that speech became something
we easily put aside. We cheered the dog on in white
puffs of breath when he took off after a startled rat,
leaning hard upon his own cornering force as he disappeared around the bulge of the crib. We rested for a
moment while the tractor roared, unburdened, and the
empty mill howled in the wind it made. Then we returned to the swing of the shovels and the cornhooks.

Time and talk disappeared on those winter days.
The gray winter light came as much out of the snow-
coated land as the sky. The wind blew hard from the

north. I bore the cold in my toes almost past the point of endurance and then pounded to the house, feet like blocks on the frozen ground, to unlace my boots and sit with my bare toes stinging in front of the heat register until my feet stopped hurting and I put them back into the cold leather and returned to the hammermill.

Between waking and the school bus waiting at the end of the driveway, or the opening of its doors in the afternoon and the dropping of darkness, there was time only, in the deepest winter, to pitch a wagonload of silage from the silo, carry it and the ground corn in two-handled baskets down the feed bunks in the west cattle yard, then repeat the process in the east cattle yard until, with the bunks full, the cattle stood contentedly chewing. We called these things "the chores," and by the time they were finished we had to get ready for either school or supper. We didn't have time to grind corn, so we did that on Saturdays, filling wagons with enough ground corn to feed the cattle for one week. I dreaded Saturday mornings, knowing the work that lay ahead—first the normal morning chores, then hooking the Five-Sixty up to the hammermill and for the rest of the morning and part of the afternoon shoveling corn into the hopper, or raking it down for a brother to shovel, in the ultimate noise of diesel roar and corncrash, and the uncaring cold of Minnesota winter and wind.

I have strong memories of the year my brothers and I ran the farm after my father's death. I tried to plant corn as straight as Dad had done, clinging to the steering wheel of the "H," my eyes fixed on the front tire, trying not to be distracted. When the corn came up,

Kevin commented that I had planted it straighter than he could have, "nearly as straight as Dad." A combiner who harvested soybeans for us lifted a rock into his header and told us: "You boys did a good job of farming but a lousy job of picking up rocks"—which was true. Spring rock picking was a job we simply neglected, though we knew better; somehow the burden of those rocks lying on the soil was too much for us to bear. I mollified the combiner, and surprised him, by attaching a carbon-arc torch to the welder and heating his header chain and straightening it, returning him to the fields within an hour when he had expected a half day lost with a trip to town for repairs.

Out of boredom, I learned to like the taste of coffee as I waited in line at the grain elevator for my turn to dump a truckload of corn. And I remember sorting cattle when it came time to sell, no longer merely advising Dad but choosing, judging, deciding for myself.

But one of the strongest memories is when the hammermill got wrecked. If it is possible for a machine to attain a mythic stature in someone's mind, then that New Holland hammermill had such status to me—in its noise, its power, its simple brute presence, in the way it dominated and formed so much of my time, the rhythms it imposed on my body by its demands.

There are essentially two ways to grind anything up, whether it be flour or coffee or cattle feed. The older way, called stone or grist or roller milling, crushes the grain between heavy weights. This is the way of water and windmills, the way of the Miller in Chaucer's *Canterbury Tales*. The weights in these old mills were generally huge stone wheels that ran around and around on a flat stone, slowly and inexorably grinding grain into flour.

The modern era, however, has substituted speed for weight. A hammermill is essentially an immense kitchen blender. Anyone who has ever sifted sand through a screen and swung a weight on a string understands its principles. The "hammers" are metal bars about four inches long and about three eighths of an inch thick, spaced about a half inch apart. There are several rows of these bars attached loosely to a foot-long cylinder inside the mill. When the cylinder is at rest the bars hang limp, but when the cylinder spins the bars swing outward. At their full extension they create a whirling blur of metal about twenty inches in diameter. This blur runs inside a metal screen with holes cut in it. The screen can be changed, depending on how fine or coarse you want something ground—coarse for cattle, fine for chickens.

Hammermills are light and portable. The one we had sat on two wheels and could be hooked up to a tractor and taken to where grain needed to be ground. It was designed to run off a 540-RPM power-take-off (PTO) on a tractor. The PTO was hooked directly to a pulley on the mill about two feet in diameter. A wide belt ran from this pulley to a much smaller one, perhaps six to eight inches in diameter, giving a three- or four-to-one reduction ratio and increase in speed. This meant the hammers whirled at about 2000 RPM, or thirty to thirty-five revolutions per second. A little quick calculating shows that the hammers moved between ninety and one hundred and twenty miles per hour. Anything that fell into them literally exploded, and didn't escape until it was small enough to be forced through the screen.

When we ground corn for the cattle, we took this thing to a corncrib and shoveled corn into a hopper, which carried it up and dropped it into the mill. If you can imagine the explosion of one ear of corn hitting those whirling hammers, and then magnify that into a steady stream of ears, dozens at a time, falling into the mill, you have an idea of the power of the thing, the sense of something huge, terrible, barely contained. If you can further imagine shoveling corn into this all of a winter Saturday, sometimes in thirty-below weather, you have a sense of the mythical stature of the machine in my imagination.

But beyond even its power was my sense of the hammermill's sheer necessity. Without it, ear corn was useless as feed. Without it, the cattle couldn't eat. Thus the machine contained, in a sense, both an economic and a moral imperative. It defined and focused all the responsibilities, all the reasons for work, on the farm.

Our hammermill had a bent PTO shaft. Because of this, we had to be careful when pulling it. The two parts of the shaft couldn't telescope beyond the bend. If we made too short a turn, the shaft would compress until it hit that bend and then, with no place to go, it would wreck something. This is precisely what one of my brothers did. He turned too short, and the PTO shaft caught at the bend. The force of the turn pushed the entire mill back toward the feed tank, knocking the pulleys eight inches out of line, cocking the bearings, twisting and buckling the heavy angle iron of the frame.

The emotions I felt when Joel told me what had

happened and I went and stared at the absolute ruin between the wheels are hard to define. I hadn't truly come to grips with Dad's death yet, and surely those long Saturdays of working in rhythm with him, of knowing what he was going to do before he did it, not because of any mind reading but simply because the task demanded it, because we were working toward the same end—surely those Saturdays were somehow mixed in with the quiet of my heart as I looked at that twisted metal and the paint flecks that had been forced from it as it bent.

It wasn't just that we had two feedings left in the wagons and I had twenty-four hours to find a solution. It was that the hammermill was indestructible. Like any other myth, it was never perfect, always problematic, but we were always able to patch it up—brazing sheet metal on holes worn through the augers, replacing the hammers, pulling and replacing bearings. It required frequent fixing, but it had never not ground a load of feed when we needed it.

In the numb silence of our stares as Joel and Colin and I looked at it, what we felt was this: With Dad gone, we had wrecked the hammermill. We had gone beyond mere mistake, beyond even disaster. We had done the impossible.

I've never met a farmer who didn't own a Handyman, or highlift, jack. My father used them for everything—stretching wire, pulling up fence posts, mounting equipment onto tractors, straightening bent metal. They can hoist things four feet into the air. That high, of course, they become extremely unstable and are susceptible to

"self jacking"; in grade school I was once knocked nearly unconscious when I tried to let down the front end of
a tractor myself. Dad yelled at me from across the yard
to stop, but I had helped to jack the tractor up and was
too sure of myself. I clicked the jack into the let-down
position and pushed down on the handle. Suddenly the
whole weight of the tractor pushed back against me and
my hand slipped. In an instant the handle was swinging
wildly up and down as the weight clicked the pins in and
out. The handle caught me on the jaw, and I lay there,
half-conscious, the handle a blur above me, as the tractor slowly and by itself descended, and Dad came running over to pick me up.

A Handyman jack seemed our best chance for
straightening the hammermill. The metal was too thick
to heat or bend with a crowbar, and there was no room
to swing a sledge hammer. But as we tried to fit the jack
in, using various angles and bases, trying it with and
without a log chain, the problem proved more and
more intractable. Either there wasn't enough room to
work the lever, or else the base of the jack slipped off
the iron. We tried for at least an hour, until we had to
do chores.

I returned to the hammermill after supper, and in
the faint yellow light of the Five-Sixty's rear bulb, I sat
on the hitch and stared into the shadows at the wild,
tangled angles of the metal. I didn't move. I didn't try
anything. I simply sat there, partly despairing and partly
believing there had to be a way. But everything I imagined failed. No matter how the jack might be inserted,
something interfered. I sat there beyond reason or
sense, and when I went to bed, that metal was still an-

gled behind my eyelids, as if it had become my own veins, the branchings and bendings of my blood.

The next morning I woke with the hammermill still on my mind. We could feed the cattle this morning, but unless I could fix the machine by about three in the afternoon, we would be forced to have the elevator in town grind feed for us or to take the hammermill to the welding shop. In retrospect these options don't seem that drastic to me, but at the time I felt hugely responsible. The machine was broken. The cattle depended on it. It was my job to fix it. It was my job. I felt an urgency unlike anything I'd ever felt before.

In a certain state, metal can look pained, and when I looked at the mill before we did the morning chores I saw that look—the silver, fevered luster where the molecules had stretched on the outside of the bends. I felt again, when I saw the incredible damage, a sinking feeling of incompetence. Nothing had changed, no solution had been revealed overnight.

We did the chores, emptying the wagons into the feed bunks, and I found myself sitting alone again on the hitch. But barely had I sat down when one of the most powerful changes in perception I've ever experienced occurred to me. For just a moment when I looked into the twisted frame it was precisely as it had been the night before. Then, in a flash, my vision reversed itself, and I saw the solution. What had been in one moment distorted and impossible became in the next completely clear and simple, the vectors of force direct and straight, the placement of the jack exact.

Only it was a different jack. Whether I saw the

space between the frame and the mill where I could fit a hydraulic jack first, or imagined using a hydraulic jack and then saw where it could fit, I don't know. Whatever happened, it was an instantaneous and complete revolution in my perception—so complete that I couldn't even see the complications any more. There, right before me, I could see the precise point to place a hydraulic jack—backward, with its base against the metal to be straightened—and I could see exactly how its force would act upon the iron to unbend it.

It was stunningly simple. I went to the pickup for the five-ton hydraulic jack we kept there. I placed it in the spot I'd seen, tightened the oil-release valve, inserted the handle, and worked the lever. Just as I'd seen in my mind, the jack sighed outward, locked against the bent angle iron and then, slowly and without effort, straightened the entire mill.

When I finished, except for three or four creases in the angle iron, everything looked normal. The PTO shaft ran straight into the bearing, the pulleys aligned, the mill sat perpendicular on the frame. I looked down the pulleys, not believing the belt could run straight between them. There had to be more to this. I reached in and turned the big pulley by hand. Inside the mill I heard the hammers swing up and drop. I stared at what I'd done, almost afraid of it. Finally I climbed onto the tractor, started the engine, and, full of doubt, slowly pulled back the PTO lever.

The hammers clinked and rattled as the large pulley revolved, transferring its power to the small one that spun the mill. In an instant the familiar howl of the spinning hammers straightening on their centrifugal force came out of the metal and a puff of corn dust rose from the dust collector. I stared at the machine, expecting to hear some awful crash of metal against metal, some note of high destruction, or expecting to see the belt suddenly ride off the edge of the pulley and flop to the ground.

Nothing happened. I opened the Five-Sixty's throttle halfway. The diesel engine built to a roar, the mill howled and thrummed, the metal resonated—all of it familiar, all of it completely normal. I jerked the throttle down. Blue exhaust streamed from the muffler and the noise of working machinery enveloped me, like a loud, blue, smoky miracle.

In some ways even now that moment seems endowed with more than ordinary possibilities. I have since learned, for instance, how incredibly difficult it can be to align two pulleys that have been misaligned, and I realize that the chances of my straightening the hammermill simply by sticking a jack in there and unbending the metal were miniscule at best. At the time, however, I could actually envision how the metal would unbend. Cognitively, much could be made of this, I suppose: the ability of the mind to see a whole situation at once, the effects of emotional stress in sharpening our thinking. But I think something else played a part.

Dad used to say, when we were jabbering at a job, that if we worked more and talked less, we'd get more done. When a hammermill is running, talk is impossible. Yet by the work of that hammermill, and by other endless tasks we performed in silence, I learned my father's life. I learned, in silence, how his muscles worked, the rhythms of his breathing, how cold crept through the soles of his boots, the ways, finally, that he responded to the world and its pleasures and difficulties.

I won't get mystical—though I'm tempted to—and say he was there guiding me as I tried to fix the hammermill. Yet in a completely real and nonmystical way, he was. In a sense I finished for him a small part of his life that he died too soon to finish. My brothers and I had learned the work of his life so completely that when he died we simply took it over, took over the care of his love—for the land, for the cattle—in a paradoxical way even for us. If his life was both distinct from the farm and yet part of it, if the farm belonged to him as he belonged to it, if we hear in that word its immense, lonely, loving echo: to be-long—to long for, to yearn for, to feel such love that being cut off from a person or a place is to be cut off from your very self—then what my brothers and I did in the year we ran the farm after his death was to love in his place, to care in his place, to live in his place, to *belong* for him.

When the hammermill was ruined I had within me the way he looked at things, the ways he worked and approached problems. Out of that, and out of my own mind, something simple and whole flashed forth from complication. Perhaps I had, as with welding, surpassed him. He wasn't inclined toward hydraulic jacks, and I'm not sure he would have seen the solution, and certainly he wouldn't have felt the desperation I did and have been driven by it. But if I saw a solution that he wouldn't have, still, in that other sense, he did see it. I saw it through him and because of him; he saw it through and because of me.

My own children, as I write this, are thirteen and eleven and seven. I am sure that I know them better than my father knew me when I was their age. He was a father of the fifties and sixties. Raising children, along with maintaining the house and doing indoor things, was primarily my mother's job, while he did the work of the farm. He recognized and honored the difficulties of my mother's position; she says he once came in from an exhausting day outside, the heat and humidity unbearable, drenched with sweat, needing water, to find her dealing with several crying children, the preparations for a meal scattered on the kitchen counters, the unnerving chaos of family. He removed his straw hat, soaked through with sweat, filled a glass with water from the tap, drank it, and turned to her. "I swear, I'd rather have my job than yours," he said.

A simple statement, but it redeemed and honored her, and she never forgot it. It was, in her own words, one of the nicest things he ever said to her. And so it is that the powerful words in a relationship are not the words of romance and ease, not even the words of passion and fervency, but the words that come in weariness, to dignify and give meaning to another's weariness.

Male and female roles were sharply defined in our family, as they were in most families during that time. My father was not as involved in the lives of his young children as I, a father of the nineties, feel I ought to be. Yet as I grew older I began to know my father better and better—not because he mellowed and joined my world, but because he expected me to join his. We didn't sit down and have heart-to-heart talks. We fed cattle. We dug post holes. We shoveled snow away from the windbreak and fences. We cleaned barns and ground corn. Much of this work we did without speaking.

I know my own children as well as I do because I enter their worlds. I play games with them, read their books, talk about their lives, go to their soccer games. As they grow older, however, I struggle to find ways to let them enter my world, a thing my father did so easily and naturally with his children—though we often grumbled about it.

The shelves of the parenting sections of bookstores are filled with titles telling modern parents how to know their children, how to interpret their moods and signals. My father, I think, was not so concerned with that. He was more concerned with his children knowing him.

I don't believe in a "work ethic"—that work equates with goodness. Yet I'm quite sure that when work is performed by parents and children together toward a necessary and ultimately moral good—for instance, so that animals don't starve, or so that a family can make a living and stay together—it serves to pass on the story and meaning of the parents' lives more effectively than anything else. Out of the years I worked around that hammermill, some meaning, some family culture, some true and real myth extending beyond my own life and embedded deeply in my father's, was conveyed to me. I was able to look with his eyes and think with his mind—and then with my own mind solve a new problem, rejuvenating in a sense my father and his thought, making his ways of knowing useful to me and my world.

My world, now, is very different from his. There

are times when I wonder whether the ways I was trained, the stories I learned through all those days of labor and wind—those silent, gripping stories—are useful in any way, and whether they can be passed on. Surely this is one of the reasons I write, to pass them on, to pass my life on, to give others—and at a very personal level, to give my children—my life, to let it belong to them. But words, I sometimes think, are a second-order form of storytelling, less powerful and direct than the silence that occurs when we simply work with someone, doing the necessary things that belong to that person's life.

Farming as we farmed was, on the other hand, a mania of work. As my brother Colin once said to me: "We did everything the hard way." I wouldn't desire my own children to have to work that hard. Yet it remains to be seen whether anything I can substitute for it will give them the part of my life they need when I am gone and something important to them kinks and bends, and lies before them utterly destroyed.

Chickens

In early May, Dad went to the hatchery in town and brought back baby chickens, and we came home from school and rushed to the brooder house. We had to contain our energy and noise before we opened the door, however, or the chicks would panic and flee over their peanut shells like butter melting in the red light of the heat lamps, becoming a mass of quivering yellow in the corner. Even though Dad nailed cardboard to the walls to round the corners out, the chicks would suffocate each other unless one of us walked over and scooped them with both hands, dozens at a time, back to the center of the brooder house.

We loved them. We loved them passionately, tenderly, inordinately. We loved the way they stood, so small, at the waterer and dipped their tiny beaks in and tilted their heads to let the water run down their throats. We loved the way they came when we knocked on the wooden board containing them, loved how they could mistake such a crude imitation for a mother they'd never known. We loved the way they disappeared, even in our small hands, if we picked them up in one palm and covered them with the other. Even though they meant more work, meant feed and water carried from the hydrant and granary all the way to the brooder house, we hardly cared. We loved them.

But baby chickens are the briefest of loves. It is hard to describe how fast white comes. They change so quickly that loving them is like holding a precious liquid in your hands and watching it drain away, and this even for a child changing so fast himself that time is like a wide, slow plain of river barely moving. For a week we were able to convince ourselves that the chicks were immutable, deserving of the inordinate affection we felt for them, but always within the yellow fluff a paling of white appeared. The down began to stiffen, and the dear, soft things upon which we had heaped our lavish praise began to turn ungainly, big-hipped, long-necked, cantankerous, and ugly.

The leghorn roosters turned ornery and stupid, the pullets merely stupid. Soon they were all outside during the day, white spots scattered among the apple orchard trees, daring to cross the driveway but fleeing back across the path of approaching cars, their instincts for safety so awry they would run out of the ditch right under the wheels of the car in order to gain the brooder house. You could never be sure, no matter how far down the ditch they were, that they wouldn't make a suicide run, necks stretched out, legs pumping like pistons out of balance, eyes eternally amazed.

The roosters strutted, crowed, their combs falling over their eyes like tilted hats on dimwitted, teenage gangsters. When I was very young they terrorized me, sending me screaming to the house, bewildered and betrayed—only a while ago I had loved them Then I discovered that if I rode my tricycle toward them they retreated, that a steady advance would cause them to lower their wings and flee disgracefully, peering back from under their combs in the hopes that pursuit would stop and they could turn and pretend to chase me off. Soon I realized it wasn't the tricycle but the bravado that frightened them, and after that I walked right toward them as they flapped their wings and made darting feints toward me until finally, chagrined by their failure to frighten, they fled, objects of my scorn.

For Dad's birthday on July 1 we always had the first chicken of the summer, three roosters freshly butchered the day before. After that the butchering continued steadily, until seventy-five chickens had been killed, dipped in scalding water to loosen their feathers, plucked, cleaned, cut into pieces, and frozen. The whole family was involved. There were always a couple of days set aside when we did the majority of them, twenty or thirty at a time, the cats meowing around our feet and the dog chasing them away, establishing his dominance as first in line for the guts.

Mom ran all the knives in the house through the knife sharpener, a white electric thing with the name *Oster* on it, containing two small spinning Carborundum wheels. She set the sharpened knives aside, filled the blue, metal canner with water and got it boiling on the stove. Then, with potholders, holding it away from her body, she carried it down to the space between the big corncrib and the machine shed, about seventy yards from the house, followed by a procession of children, one carrying the knives wrapped in newspaper, others carrying bowls of cold water in which to rinse the meat, all carrying voices that complained, complained, complained, with the monotonous repetiton of scolding jays.

Between the machine shed and the corncrib my mother met my father and his procession of complaining children, all carrying newly decapitated chickens. Holding the chickens by the legs, the adults and the older children dipped them into the hot water, swirled them around to make sure they were soaked, pulled them out, and handed them to the younger children, who began to pull the hot, wet feathers off in clumps that stuck to everything. The only fun we had out of it was trying to cover the cats with feathers, turning them half-feline, half-bird. They were always hungry, being supported only by the welfare of table scraps, otherwise earning their living as mousers—a good living for the dedicated, a patchy, mangy-fur sort of living for the lazy—and the chicken butchering was a glory for them. Dressed in their feathers, looking like fools and convicts, dragging guts away through the grass, they were jesters and clowns and pickpockets at a solemn religious festival.

Quickly a method was established. With a few chickens plucked, first Mom, then Dad, then—working down the birth order—Kevin, Renee, me, Joel, perhaps Colin, until we ran out of sharp knives—moved to butchering, while Ann, Cyndee, Marie, and Paul continued to remove feathers. We opened the chickens, slid out the glistening intestines (saving the hearts and gizzards), found the joints where thigh met body, cracked them open, separated thigh and drumstick, removed the lizard-skinned legs, cut off the wings, and sliced down the breasts to separate them from the backs and then again from the wishbones. We threw the pieces of meat into cold water, which turned pink.

Other than the work's sheer physical monotony, none of this particularly bothered me, once I got used to it. It didn't really matter that six weeks earlier I'd been holding these chickens, feeling eternal affection, didn't matter that I'd been able, by knocking on a board, to call them to me, their surrogate mother, and cover them with my fine, good hands. Love between child and chicken changes that fast and that completely. The best meal of the summer was always Dad's birthday meal, and it was always a meal of chicken, not chickens.

My Mother's
Silence

There was the blue speckled canner with its wire rack inside it, and there was the stainless steel pressure cooker, which we children trod around quietly as if it were a bomb, as in fact it was. The canner and the pressure cooker came out of the dirt basement in June, and one or the other of them sat on the stove constantly and mercilessly until August. The canner clinked and bubbled, the wire rack inside it holding quart glass jars. The pressure cooker made no sound. One was friendly, talkative, maternal, the other brooding and uncommunicative as a gunfighter. The canner's lid could be lifted, the covers of the jars checked, and we could hear them popping as they sealed. The pressure cooker gave no sign at all. We felt relief and satisfaction every time Mom, having let it cool and released the pressure, removed the lid and found that it had worked, that her timing had been right, her knowledge and memory correct.

The canner was used on high acid foods like tomatoes. Low acid foods like string beans, susceptible to
botulism, required the pressure cooker. To bring a jar of
string beans up from the basement during the winter,
and to open it and eat them, was an elemental act of
faith, like trusting one's knowledge of wild mushrooms,
for as my mother told us more than once, if they were
bad we'd never have time to find out. Certainty could
kill you. Knowledge that the pressure cooker had done
its job was always retrospective, and never remarked.

My mother has heard women thirty and forty
years younger than she speaking of the joys of putting
up their own garden, the craft and the art of home
canning. She's listened to them compare their recipes
for pickles, heard them trying to impress each other
with their knowledge and techniques, bragging of
their numbers.

"Ten quarts of tomatoes," my mother said to me.
"They talk about doing ten quarts of tomatoes, and
how fulfilling it is. I've thought of telling them. But
then I think: 'What's the use?' But I hate to listen to
them talk."

Then she went silent, and I did too.

Ten quarts of tomatoes.

My mother put up a hundred and twenty. Every
summer. She didn't have tomato plants. She had a
tomato patch. She had rows and rows of beans. Cu-
cumbers sprawled like a jungle. Cabbages thickened in
two long rows. And the corn—it wasn't even planted in
the garden but in the fields, several rows of it alongside
the taller field corn.

When my wife and I plant our small garden every spring, it takes a few hours, scraping lines in the soil with a hoe and dropping in seeds. My mother's garden took several days to plant. She sent one of us children to the barrel that held used baler twine and we knotted pieces of it together until we had a long string. She tied this to stakes that she drove into the ends of the rows, measuring so that the rows were parallel, and she planted down the taut twine. My wife and I don't need string; if we get a little crooked it doesn't matter. But if my mother got crooked, by the time she reached the end of the row one hundred feet away, the error would be magnified enough to throw the entire garden off.

Merely planting a garden that size was a big job, to say nothing of weeding it in a place where weeds grew everywhere they were allowed—in the road ditches, the grove surrounding the farmstead, crowding into the cattle yards, sneaking into the fields. The battle against weeds was never-ending. But it's the canning I want to convey here. Perhaps mere numbers, unembellished, are best:

120 quarts of tomatoes.
50 quarts of string beans.
80 quarts of sweet corn.
30 quarts of sauerkraut.
50 quarts of pickles.
70 quarts of applesauce.

And those were just the crops she grew. Add the fruits she bought in wooden crates from Paul Tempel's store in town, and the numbers increase:

70 quarts of peaches.
40 quarts of cherries.
30 quarts of apricots.
20 quarts of pears.

These are numbers of necessity.

Another way to convey what canning meant to my mother is this: her ankles swelled up from standing in the hot kitchen in the humid Minnesota summers. When she could no longer bear it, she got out the red metal stool that her children sat on when they first graduated from a high chair and she sat on this at the countertop, and went on peeling and cutting.

Full jars. Empty jars. Full jars. Empty. The canning jars gleamed on shelves in the dimly lit basement, gleamed in a daily, practical way. They were Kerr, Ball, and Mason jars, their names molded on them in large cursive or block letters, in clear or light blue glass, some of them passed down from my mother's mother, my father's mother.

The jars were stacked four deep on shelves that ran from one corner of the back basement wall to the other, from floor to ceiling. The basement had a dirt floor—one of my mother's greatest embarrassments, as were the toads and salamanders we sometimes found there—and a single light bulb. We didn't play in the basement like the children in stories did, didn't go there for solitude or adventure. If we wanted those things we went outside, to the grove, the road ditches, the hayloft. We went to the basement primarily at our mother's request, to retrieve a jar of peaches or cherries for dessert, or a vegetable for a hotdish.

The light, blocked by the furnace, didn't make it around to the shelves, except at the corners. In the almost-dark we found what our mother needed, plucked it off the shelves, carried it back up the wooden steps to the kitchen. Later we carried the empty jars back down. At the end of summer, when the jars were full, the various colors of the fruits inside them—golden, red, dark purple, deep green—absorbed the light. By spring they stood open mouthed on the shelves, faintly gleaming, barely blue.

The work of canning came as the seasons came, not as something demarcated and decided, not as something chosen. It was instead as ordinary and accepted as going to school, as blizzards, as humidity in the summer, as flies on the screen door, as rain.

First we sat on chairs on the lawn, bowls of unshelled peas before us, and we cracked the pods and dropped four or five puny peas into another bowl where they rolled around like planets in a sunless, awry system.

Next came beans, easier than peas: crack the stems or cut them, rinse in colanders.

Then it was a frenzy of canning, with one crop ripening before the other was finished, the summer consumed with filling jars, each crop with a different method and way. Necessity drove my mother to pull from the land, and preserve, with the drudgery of labor and the intelligence of memory and experimentation, a richness of taste and texture almost as varied as the old long-grass prairie itself. Summer was a tapestry, in time, of colors and smells and tastes, the rich steam of one crop having barely left the kitchen before the next filled it.

Tomatoes were deceptive, seemingly rich and full of promise, but with so much water in them that they compressed forever. My mother pushed and pushed them, her fingers going down into the jars, coming out, going in, working the pulp in and the air out, a sinkful of tomatoes, their skins removed in the hot water, reduced to a quart—a hundred and twenty sinkfuls.

And against the bright red of the tomatoes was the waxen yellow of the corn. It's one thing to pick and husk and remove the silk from a few ears of corn for a summer barbecue, but it's another to stand in rows stretching down a field and fill five-gallon pails with ears and carry them to the pickup and dump them and go back for more, until the ears are heaped to the sideboards, and then to drive to the house and begin to remove the husks and silk and put the naked ears into buckets again, or paper sacks, and take them into the house, and to have the easiest part of the job done.

We stood in the kitchen with sharp knives, slicing off kernels, letting them drop onto the counter. My mother used the corn-cutting board, essentially a reverse plane—a wooden board with a metal blade jutting out from a slit. It was fast and efficient. She swept the ears back and forth without paying the kind of attention one had to with a knife. But because it didn't require attention, it was dangerous. Every summer, at least once, she'd get distracted—a child complaining, a fight, a request, or outright weariness—and she'd push a slippery ear forward, trying to remove the last row of kernels, and sweep the tip of her finger right into the blade, and a flap of skin would fall like a bright, violent kernel onto the pile of corn below.

But the worst was cabbage. Cabbages grew from that rich, southern Minnesota soil like immense mushrooms, layered thickly leaf within leaf, an extravagance of vegetable. Yet I imagine my mother seeing them and thinking there could be too much of God's bounty, if it came in the wrong form. She had no choice but to plant a vegetable that yielded as much mass as cabbages yielded. But all she could do to preserve what we didn't immediately eat was to turn it into sauerkraut, and canning sauerkraut was like canning complaint, dissatisfaction, dissent. We children all hated sauerkraut. Every year she adjusted the recipe, trying to find a solution of brine and vinegar that her children would tolerate. She was never successful.

Each summer the cabbages swelled large and full, packed with promise, yet obscene and ironic, and each winter we children complained all the way down the basement steps and all the way back up when we were sent down to bring up a jar of sauerkraut, and we ate it complaining, never considering, as children never consider anything, that Mom had hurt and grown weary making this for us. Perhaps our complaining was as necessary and ironic, in its own way, as cabbages, and as her work and love.

At the auction sale the summer after Dad died, my mother's canning jars sat on the back of a bale rack in cardboard boxes, and they were auctioned off box-by-box to neighbors and strangers, along with everything else that had made up life on the farm. There was much to regret at that auction sale, but Mom was not sorry to see her canning jars go.

After Dad's death, land prices, and rentals with them, went high. A couple of Mom's children were on their own, and Social Security helped with those who weren't. No longer was it necessary to invest every last possible penny back into the farm. These things combined to make the work of canning unnecessary. Mom could buy canned goods. My father's death, in another irony, made the accumulated wealth of their life together suddenly available to her.

I could create a sentimental image here, of how she watched her jars being auctioned away, and how she had poured her love and life into them, and how they symbolized, as they were carried away, the emptiness of her life now. That image would be partly true, that sentiment more than sentimentality. But it wouldn't account for how life can be too full, and how there are degrees and varieties of emptiness in life, and not all of them are black, not all of them depressing.

Surely, as Mom heard the empty jars clink in the boxes as neighbors carted them away, as she realized that the blue speckled canner would not this summer or any other bubble on the stove, the pressure cooker would not brood like a bomb, she must have felt the kind of emptiness that drags upon the heart, feels like lead in the chest, and is the body's question: "What do I do now?" But she must have also felt the kind of emptiness that lifts the heart like a balloon, the emptiness of cutting the shackles of duty and need, and that is the spirit's question: "What *can* I do now?"

Silence, like emptiness, has many forms. There is the silence of resentment, the silence of awe, the silence of anger, of not understanding, of peace, of coming storm, of rock and water, of crowds and of solitude. My mother's silence around young women who brag of their delight in home canning is, I believe, a silence of wisdom and experience, which includes and resolves other silences.

Canning shaped my mother's life in ways that the young women who think of it as a craft will never know. And my mother shaped the culture of our family by canning, took the way we made our living and gave it variety, texture, consistency, taste. She reproduced and commented on all sides of life—the mellowness of peaches in syrup, the tang of apricots, the sweetness of pears, the strong bite of tomatoes, the earthiness of peas and beans, the almost sexual mustiness of corn, the ethereal aroma of strawberry preserves, and the ocean brininess of sauerkraut.

Children want culture to be easy, and they want it all to be good. Adults come to realize that culture is hard work, requiring constant attentiveness, sweat, and care. Still, culture isn't wasted on children. I think that if I had a jar of my mother's sauerkraut now, which I hated as a child, I would enjoy its taste, nuanced and

unique, a specific summer's cabbage, a specific summer's work. Having learned that life is often bitter or
sour as well as sweet, I'd finally enjoy the taste of my
mother's sauerkraut, because I'd recognize it.

My mother's silence in the presence of young
women babbling about the joys of home canning is the
silence of the artist in the presence of mere craft's
bravado and one-upmanship. It would be Michelangelo's silence were he to come down from the Sistine
Chapel's ceiling to find a group of aristocrats for whom
painting is a diversion and a pastime speaking of how
fulfilling they find it.

Michelangelo, his back aching from lying on
planks, his arm so sore he can hardly hold it up, might
listen to the group try to impress each other. He might
think to comment and list his own achievements. But
what could he say that they would understand? Painting has shaped his life. It's not something he does; it's
who he is. To comment to the chattering aristocrats
would be to cheapen his life, and reduce it.

The ceiling has to speak for itself, Adam and Eve
and the hand of God, spirit and body, passion, pain, defeat, redemption, life and death. And the dirt basement, so much more ordinary but almost as magnificent, has to speak for itself—the shelves of jars, empty
and full and empty, the blue, daily glimmering in the
dim light, the work my mother did so that her family
could taste life and live, all that sensuality and richness.

My mother never thought of herself as an artist, but
her silence is the silence of an artist who won't comment
on her work, who trusts it to speak, though it may take

years for the message to be heard. She won't defend her
life or work, and so make them less than they are. Her
canning enriched life and commented on it in subtle,
powerful ways for her small, important audience, her
children. We heard, even if we didn't acknowledge the
hearing—and that is disappointing and fulfilling enough.
What else is there to say, what else to prove or defend?

The Conversation
of the Roses

After church on Sunday mornings we parked in front of my grandmother's house and piled out of the car. Under the shade of her weeping willow littering the yard with twigs, in the hot stillness of the July cicadas' cries, within the slow, suffused quiet of a small town after church on a day already humid, we filed up the narrow sidewalk, through the screen door, and into the tiny kitchen—the gray linoleum floor, the old heat registers, the painted cupboards. Some of us found our way to the cool cement basement, where we played with a plastic bowling game. Others slouched on the living room furniture, reading the Sunday paper while the adults visited.

In time my mother would say, "Let's go look at the roses," or my grandmother would say, "Do you want to see the roses?" and the two of them walked back out of the house, my mother in her Sunday clothes—high heels, lipstick, nylons, dress—my grandmother in a plain cotton dress that fell to her calves, thick black shoes. Beginning at the front of the house, they started, going counterclockwise, close together, stopping for long periods, talking quietly, pointing to things I couldn't see.

My grandmother always had her arms crossed on her chest—thin arms, thin gray hair, thin cotton dress. A car might drift down the street, the neighbors behind its windshield lifting their hands in cursory waves. The two women, mother and daughter, didn't notice. They walked absorbed in the roses blooming along the water-stained foundation, the world at their backs, mysterious in their silence and self-containment. The cicadas chanted, the willow sighed in the heat. On the narrow sidewalk my mother's high heels clicked and stopped, clicked and stopped, and my grandmother's thick heels softly chucked.

The roses grew all around the house, yellow, white, red, budded and blooming in the high heat of summer, having survived their winter dormancy. In the fall we hauled straw bales into town for my grandmother. She turned the roses into the soil, and we placed the bales over them, then removed them in the spring. In her garden dress and hat, a trowel in her hand, she knelt and set them upright again, packing the rich, warming soil around their roots, fertilizing and watering them.

I sometimes left the pleasant basement or the funny papers and stood at a distance, watching the two women, afraid to ask what they saw, afraid to break their spell. Curiosity demands questions; mystery prohibits them, is felt as question and answer both, and speaks from and points to silence.

This was the opposite of my mother's canning, work done, care taken, unnecessarily, for beauty's sake alone. Other flowers required tending, but only roses seemed to require this looking, this study and quiet conversation. My mother bought geraniums and chrysanthemums in little pods from a greenhouse, and planted them, and they grew. Tulips appeared all by themselves. The peony bushes along our driveway bloomed as violently as fire and scattered a circle of red, wilted flames beneath them through which the new, white pullets strutted and scratched. The honeysuckle climbing the wall outside our living room grew without our noticing, until it attracted summer hummingbirds, which we called to each other to watch.

Only roses seemed to need, beyond mere care, attention. This past winter I visited my sister Ann and her husband in California. Tom showed me a bush outside their house with what looked like rosebuds on it, but I had to ask him what it was. Roses to me were always delicate, low-growing things, that had to be urged from the ground, treated with utmost consideration. This bush in California was a sprawling, anarchic thing that, Tom told me, he had to trim twice a year or it would grow over the garage.

In Minnesota, on the other hand, growing roses is a complete thing, like exquisite lyric poetry or like painting in oils, and like these it is something close to foolishness, so much effort for so little product. My mother and grandmother had to encourage all their roses' potential in the small time of warmth between the iron soils of spring and fall—so little time to bring the plants from dormancy, to set their roots, to get them growing. But as soon as the roses began to grow, the women had to carefully prune them back, directing the plants' potential into only the strongest shoots and buds—and they never knew for sure whether they were truly listening to the plants, cooperating with their growing and their potential, or imposing their own will and desires.

Not even when the willow littered the lawn and the cicadas made the whole, hot morning sway and rock in late July did my grandmother know for sure. When the buds burst from the heat into flowers, they were so folded together, so fragrant and defiant, so insistent upon themselves, so beautiful, that, like an ode or a Grecian urn, they stopped time, they were their own truth. But my grandmother could never know for sure that there wasn't another form the rose's truth could have taken, other buds that might have bloomed, a deeper, richer beauty.

So she gathered her daughter to share the mystery with her, to ritualize and to try to understand it, and they walked heads down and quietly, appreciative and critical both, and they engaged the whole, timeless world—the lusty, shrill cicadas, and the willow discarding its branches, and the grandchildren who had left their bowling game in the basement to wait on the sidewalk to go home so that time could resume—they engaged them all in the quiet speaking of, the attendance upon, the conversation of, the roses.

My Grandmother's Bones

My grandmother stood at the top of the road ditch, unmoving. At my mother's words I turned around, puzzled. I stopped bounding through the tall, un-mowed grass of the ditch, stopped swinging my ice cream bucket, stopped feeling the luxury of gravity pulling me down, making me feel like a deer for the few bounds it took to descend the ditch to where the elder-berries drooped like heavy hearts. I turned and stared at my grandmother, at her thin legs and the way she wasn't moving, at how she stood on the road and didn't come down.

I hated elderberries with the visceral intensity of a child who has identified his least favorite food. Before the federal government disallowed it, St. Michael's school, the Catholic grade school I attended, saved money on lunches by cooking what was at hand—a side of beef donated by a farmer, or locally grown apples

and tomatoes. One of these money-saving foods was elderberries.

Elderberries are inedible in their natural state, tiny
bombs of juice that explode between your teeth and,
like a desiccating wind, dry everything instantly, so that
even the roof of your mouth puckers. Cooked with
sugar and pectin, however, elderberries produce a dark
purple, glutinous mass that can be poured over an oat-
meal crust, named "Elderberry Crunch," and foisted
upon unsuspecting first graders as dessert.

Even now the memory of Elderberry Crunch is a
hurtful thing to me. Philosophically I can admire those
church volunteers and the hard work they did, and I
can appreciate the localness and uniqueness of a dessert
made from the spontaneous products of the land, the
rare, wild flavor, and I can understand why many of my
classmates loved Elderberry Crunch. But laying philoso-
phy aside, I've never grown up in my attitude toward
Elderberry Crunch the way I did with sauerkraut.

I detested Elderberry Crunch from the moment I
first saw it lifted, dripping, off the large aluminum pan
in St. Michael's serving line and placed, sagging, on my
brown, plastic tray, and I hated its thick, syrupy smell as
I walked to the long tables where my companions sat,
and I dreaded it for the entire meal, as if it were a
swollen, purple eye glaring at me from the plate. I finally forced myself to eat it—for it was either that or risk
the wrath of the nuns who watched the cafeteria with
unsympathetic eyes and who insisted that a starving
child in India would love to have our food and who, on
that basis, severely punished anyone who stuffed it in a
milk carton or tried to give it to a friend. I gagged and

choked, and drinking milk didn't help, nor did holding my nose.

My grandmother lived under the same, proud rule of frugality and independence that St. Michael's school had institutionalized. While I don't know that she ever committed Elderberry Crunch, her food sins did include Green Tomato Pie, made from tomatoes that hadn't ripened before frost, which she served at the Thanksgiving meals we had at her place, and which I made the mistake of trying once. What she did with elderberries was make preserves, so every summer we'd gather to help her pick them.

Picking elderberries was not nearly as bad as eating them. Picking involved August heat and mosquitoes, and the plucking of tiny berries, one by one, from the clusters where they nodded. The delicate stem usually came off with the berry and so had to be picked off again before the berry could be dropped in the bucket. (There was nothing worse than the extra crunch in Elderberry Crunch caused by missed stems.)

My mother and her sister Phyllis gathered several of their children and, along with my grandmother, drove to a spot where elderberries grew. We sulked in the car all the way down the dusty roads, staring out the window as if the land itself had something to do with our misery—as in a way it did—or we fought with a sibling until my mother threatened to stop the car. But when the bushes hove into view, deeply purple, all of that changed.

No matter how much the human body itself responds with aversion to the sweat and itch of harvest, the human heart counters with song and gladness.

Even when the body hates the fruit of the harvest, for the heart it's like a coming-home, a forgiveness—like a remembering, after long drifting and prodigality, that the world is good and that life is generous. Everything is offered; all you have to do is forget your stinginess, your own tight hoarding of effort, your puckering of soul, and take. It requires an opening-up to generosity, a willingness to accept and be glad.

For children this willingness comes spontaneously, but lasts only about half an hour into the actual harvest, before the body's aversion gains primacy over the heart. But when we first saw the elderberries, saw that we had beaten the birds to them, saw the wide purple palms of fruit nodding in gravity, we forgot our fights and sullenness and saw only the gift of the world.

We piled out of the car and leaped down the ditch, brothers and sisters and cousins, plastic pails knocking against our knees, crying out like birds at the size of the clusters, forgetting our past complaints and coming work, feeling only that all things in the world were free, that we were free, fleeing the cramped car and flying like birds down, down, over the road ditch grass, toward the berries nodding their yeses.

I was almost to the bush when my mother's voice stopped me. A rich clump swayed over my head, within reach, and I was almost to it, within the shadowed cool of the leaves already. Then my mother called my name, and I turned from the harvest to see what she wanted. I was in sixth grade, the oldest child there. Already, in this brief pause, my younger brothers and sisters were bending branches into their hands.

"Help your grandmother down the ditch," my mother said quietly, with a tone of regret in her voice.

It puzzled me. Help my grandmother? That made no sense. When did my grandmother need help in anything? As far as I knew she'd always lived alone, fierce in her independence, like some lone and weathered tree. The idea of helping her was incomprehensible.

I followed my mother's eyes. There, at the edge of the road, holding her own plastic bucket, stood my grandmother, her cotton dress hanging in the still air, looking down at the ditch sloping at her feet. She stared at that tiny ditch—which I had just bounded down in three leaps—the way a novice skier might stare at a steep, tree-filled slope. Her black shoes, unmoving, just touched the long grass.

She said nothing, asked nothing. She wasn't aware that Mom had spoken to me. In her silence lay all her defeat and refusal to be defeated, this monstrosity of gravity leering up at her, mocking, and she about to dare it rather than ask for help. She shuffled toward it on legs, I suddenly saw, too thin—like sticks, I saw, like straw. When had her legs turned to straw?

I looked at my mother again, but she simply looked back at me, wordless. I realized nothing more could be said, that silence had to be maintained. I couldn't even ask what kind of help was required, what form it was supposed to take.

I trudged reluctantly up the ditch, trying to decide what I was going to do when I reached my grandmother. She saw me coming and stopped moving, recognizing what was passing, but we were all—I knew it instinctively—involved in this pact to hide from each other our knowledge that any of this was necessary. It was to look like courtesy only, respect. Even as I tried to come to grips with my grandmother's sudden, revealed infirmity, I was forbidden to acknowledge it.

I reached her, stood for a moment before her. Our eyes didn't meet. Nothing passed between us but mutual determination to make this something other than her defeat and the earth's wide mockery. I was no Boy Scout. I had never been trained in helping the elderly cross streets. I knew nothing about offering elbows, about being a stable, moving handrail.

And I wasn't accustomed to touching my grandmother. She loved her grandchildren, but not in an effusive way. Even her love was dignified and independent. I looked at her for a moment, then took a brief, clumsy step to the side and reached out and grabbed her arm above the elbow.

My plan, if I had one at all, was to march her down the hill. To that end I gripped her hard, as if she was a bale of hay I was wrestling into position.

My grip went to the bone.

To the bone. My fingers passed through the wilted skin and muscle of her upper arm as if they were passing through something overripe and wasted. I expected muscle like my own, like my father's or mother's, swollen with strength, to resist my grip. In church I'd seen the loose skin on the arms of old women, but I'd never touched it like this before, and now my fingers sank into it and closed around my grandmother's narrow bone.

I was shocked, then revolted.

Immediately I felt shame for that revulsion.

Both emotions hit me at once, like a lightning stroke, in the time it takes to almost jerk your hand away from the touch of something grotesque and to will yourself, even as your muscles are contracting, to keep your hand where it is, to loosen nothing. I maintained my hard grip on my grandmother's frail, awful bone, my hand sunk in her sagging flesh, and marched her, stiff as a wooden soldier, down the road ditch grade.

She couldn't be hurried. Time seemed interminable. Her feet reached out, sought the earth, as tenuously as a snake's tongue seeks vibrations in the air. I held on, held on, until we finally reached the level bottom. Then I withdrew my hand as quickly as I could from the grave of her flesh and turned her over to my mother.

Unable to think, trying to pretend that all was fine, I went to the elderberries and began to pick them mechanically, one by one. Hours later, even with my hands stained purple and sweat washing out of my pores, my grandmother's bones hadn't forsaken my nerves or abandoned my skin.

Old Waters

Not family only, but land too, has its stories. When you make your living off the land and belong to it, you come to feel it as something with force and presence, and as a past that is not dead but an ongoing narrative in which you partake. I grew up on flat prairieland, so flat my father used to remark that you could stand on your hat and see ten miles—one of his typical dry and understated jokes; it took me years of hearing him say this to realize that if you stood on your hat you'd crush it and be standing on the ground.

I knew flat land. We used to climb the silo with binoculars to watch the Fourth of July fireworks in Redwood Falls ten miles away, and from the haymow door we could look across miles and miles of snow-dusted fields or shimmering green corn. Yet I never understood the essence of the northern prairie, or felt its deepest power, until I went to the source of its story. At the border of Minnesota and North Dakota, near Moorhead and Fargo, lies the most minimalist of all possible landscapes, a place with which not even the simplicity of the sea can compete, a place where flatness has been perfected.

It is called the Red River Valley of the North. The land was formed by the ancient, glacial Lake Agassiz, which itself was formed when the Wisconsin glaciation receded, and what it left to the modern eye is a landscape spare and austere, which distills and magnifies the experience of prairie. Born a flatlander, I knew when I first went to the Red River Valley that even flat land has its nuances and shadings, but I found none there. There, the miles are flat, the acres are flat, the square yards are flat—not a single rise, not a single dip or depression. The earth has been planed.

An art instructor at the college where I currently teach, near the Black Hills, once told me that his students have trouble understanding perspective. Yet when I was introduced to perspective in grade school art class, I understood it immediately and instinctively, as a lesson taught by my landscape every summer day— the level cornfields with my father's perfectly straight rows diminishing nearly to a point up near the county road three-eighths of a mile away.

Yet I was totally unprepared for the astonishing, the shocking flatness of the Red River Valley of the North. From the time we're children, all of us, no matter where we live, have been prepared, by the romancers of space and view, for the experience of mountains, which, when I first saw them as a young man outside of Denver, disappointed me because they weren't as magnificent in reality as the photographs I'd seen.

A camera, however, cannot capture the power and eerieness of the prairie, cannot capture the visceral experience of flatness. The first time I visited the Red River Valley, friends took me for a drive to see the country. As we crossed railroad tracks I saw them converge in perfect perspective in the distance. Down where they converged a grain elevator stuck above the prairie, the whole elevator, top to bottom.

"What's that town down there?" I asked.

My friend named it, though I've forgotten the name.

"How far is it?"

"Oh, fifteen miles," he said, matter-of-factly.

One's sense of space is different on flat land than it is in rolling or mountainous land. On the land of the Red River Valley, if you hold your fingers in front of you to measure the space to the horizon, you encompass the whole between thumb and forefinger held about an inch apart. You can see forever, but forever takes no seeing. In contrast, where I now live, the land sweeps down into town, then rises behind it, swaying upward into the Black Hills, cutting itself into ridges, until, in a blue magnificence of space, it culminates in Crow Peak.

It seems an immense distance—but it's all illusion. Crow Peak is about nine miles from town, not nearly as far as that grain elevator, which seemed so close, but because it is possible to mark the distance to Crow Peak, because the eye shifts and changes to take it in, it seems vast and spacious.

Straight lines don't exist and don't merge in mountains, and often the most distant thing seems the largest. In the Red River Valley of the North, however, a land of perfect perspective, where nothing obstructs your view—the most spacious landscape in the world—you can feel oddly constricted, as if space is drawing close, compressing in upon you.

Buildings and people stand "on" or "upon" the prairie, but we build houses "in" the mountains, go for hikes "into" the hills. We feel we can enter or merge with mountains, but we feel separated from the prairie, standing hard "upon" it. Even on the most isolated spot of prairie we feel visible and exposed, but mountains, even crowded ones, give a feeling of privacy.

Mountains are inherently romantic. They allow us to imagine a private, freeing, and enfolding relationship. Just as people seek solitude with a lover, so they try to claim hidden, jealous places in mountains, not for the solitude itself—which can be immense on the prairie, yet people don't usually build their dream homes there—but for the romance mountain solitude provides.

The major fear inherent in mountain landscapes, accompanying the freedom of hiddenness, is the fear of becoming lost. As much as we want our hiding places, we also want to find our way back. Our experience of mountains is always tinged with the fear that we could become lost, and the deeper we go into mountains—the more we seek the fullness of privacy and freedom they provide—the greater grows the accompanying fear.

On the prairie, however, where we stand out, self-contained and separate, freedom is made manifest by the journey. We seldom worry about becoming lost on the prairie. We can always trace a straight line, and even should our ways turn crooked, chances are we can see our destination, down where the tracks converge, down where the rainbow ends.

On the other hand, this freedom of movement has its own accompanying fears. The first is that movement will stop, and we will be stuck "out in the middle of nowhere." "Nowhere" in this phrase means a flat road converging to a point in the distance, and nothing but sky all around—and if you don't believe this, check out what nowhere looks like in the next commercial advertising a car that won't leave you stranded there.

Yet along with the fear of being stranded on the prairie, in a place that even Dorothy in *The Wizard of Oz* had to learn to call "home," is the opposite fear of not being held at all, of being so disconnected, so much "upon" the surface, that you can be swept away. Part of the power of *The Wizard of Oz* is that it expresses both these fears—of being stuck in a nowhere place, and of being disconnected from place entirely.

Classical in its simplicity, the prairie's whole character is revealed in the visual tension between the arch of the sky and the plane of the earth, and in their corresponding forces, the wind trying to sweep you away, gravity barely holding you down.

On the prairie, surprises always come from the sky. When you can stand on your hat and see ten miles, you learn not to anticipate surprises from the land. In the mountains, every step might yield a new view. Peaks rise and fall behind each other, valleys open up, animals suddenly appear. But on the prairie anything approaching or approached will first be seen in the smallness of perspective and will only gradually grow large.

Only from the sky can anything come fast and large enough to startle and surprise, destroying the rules of perspective. With its potential for chaos and sudden change, the sky hangs immensely over the visually predictable prairie, upon which it is nearly impossible to find adequate hiding places. When I was about nine years old I was pounding nails in the lumber pile fifty yards from the house when something—an overbearing silence, a quality of light, a dash of cold air against my neck—caused me to glance up. I saw a black cloud looming behind the grove on the western horizon, perspective eliminated by its size, distance swallowed by its speed. I dropped my hammer and ran.

The cloud—beetled, rolling, magnificent—rose over the grove, swallowing the sun and light, rising and rising, dwarfing the trees and sending a cold wind before it that rattled branches, bent trees, nearly swept me off my feet as I pounded toward the house. Then the rain hit, slamming into me with such force that I felt I would be lifted away. Gravity held, and I made it, soaking wet, to the tiny, quaking house, to watch at a window as the grove, turned to string by the power of the wind, tangled itself like seaweed in the whip and sway of water. Safe now, fear set in, and I realized just how scared I'd been, completely alone in my own yard, with the sky descending.

The prairie sky's ability to isolate a person is a theme of one of the first great prairie novels, O. E. Rölvaag's

Giants in the Earth. Since that novel was written, modern prairie dwellers, who have chosen to stay in one place on the prairie in order to utilize the soil's richness, have learned to build against and deal with the sky. As long as earth and sky remain distinct, as long as the hard line of the horizon holds, prairie dwellers feel they can withstand most storms. But the greatest storm of all on the prairie is the one that annihilates this distinction, funneling the sky down to mingle with the earth.

The tornado is mythically, primevally terrifying. Unlike other skystorms, which are diffuse and widespread, the tornado is almost human in its singularity. As self-contained as if it whirled within a skin, with a vacuum at its center, the tornado annihilates every other singularity it touches. Rather than approaching from the horizon, it drops straight down from the center of the sky, and as its vacuum forms, it literally puts a hole in the air. Its blackness is formed first of cloud but it ends as dust, and like the terrifying monsters of fairy tale, the tornado fully formed stands on the earth, with its head in the clouds.

Like a jealous, self-contained and powerful god, immensely passionate and raging, the tornado is beyond logic. It follows its own path, operates at its own whim, the sky's chaos distilled. Snake and phallus both, chthonic and Olympian, the tornado gathers all the fears and freedoms of the prairie and drives them into the human heart. Against it nothing—not gravity, not individuality—stands. Within its hollow center one can literally be blown off the land, to mingle with the sky. The only possible and tenuous refuge is to dig into the earth, to burrow like blind animals and huddle in the damp and clay.

All of these things are part of a prairie mentality, but there is one other force, incredibly ancient and powerful, that shapes the people of the northern plains. Every spring Dad summoned his sons, and we rode a bale rack out to the newly disced fields, our legs dangling over the edge, the rack bouncing and banging, to pick up the rocks that had been turned up by the plow. This was the job we left undone the year he died, but he himself never ignored it.

Every year the plow found new rocks, and every spring we picked them up. They seemed to swim upward through the earth, floating as if in a dream of time through the subsoil and clay from some calving place of rock, some dark, hard womb. Some people say that frost heaves them to the surface, others that wind erosion gradually uncovers them, but however they arrive, they arrive, no matter how carefully they have been picked up the year before.

These rocks were buried by glacier during the last Ice Age, the same glacier that carved the famous ten thousand lakes of Minnesota. In spite of the drudgery and hard work of picking up rocks, I was enthralled by the notion of handling something dropped by glaciers thousands of years ago. The rocks became a focus for my imagination, a lens through which I saw the past and present, and realized they were vastly different and yet connected.

Myth provides us with a felt sense that we are part of something larger, more mysterious and powerful than our immediate senses reveal, and it makes us realize that the time of our waking lives runs parallel to another kind of time where things exist all at once. Children are so sensitive to the gifts of myth that if adults don't provide the myths, children will turn an old, crooked tree, a hole in the ground, a decrepit building, into storied and layered places where the felt power of the world is funnelled through to them, and where time doesn't pass as running thread but as whole cloth, patterned and woven.

Glaciers, among other things, provided me with this sense. I felt them as myth—the first though certainly not the last time I have turned scientific data into felt story—and it gave meaning to my landscape, which became a palimpsest upon which I could read, if I looked carefully, the signs of forces so great they bordered on the mystical. Picking rocks out of the fields was an immediate and personal connection to a different time and a force beyond imagination. In digging out the rocks we belonged to that force. Even if I hated the work, I knew I was undoing the work of a glacier, and it made me a part of that great thing. I felt time not as something day-to-day but as continuous and whole, as if the smell of mastodon remained on the rocks we hoisted out of the ground and threw onto the bale rack. And perhaps it did.

The story of the glaciers on the northern plains is wonderful and complicated. The Red River is one of the few rivers in the continental United States that flows north, draining eventually into Hudson Bay. This is a minor curiosity today, but in geologic time this northward flow of the Red River is crucial to explaining the land-scape that shaped me.

On the freeway near Fargo, North Dakota, a small sign informs travellers that they are passing over the north/south continental divide. In truth, there are several different places on the continent where north-flowing waters are separated from south-flowing ones, the line not nearly as strict as the east/west division, since all the waters eventually make it to either the Pacific or Atlantic oceans. Near Fargo, however, this sign makes no immediate sense at all. Flat plains stretch endlessly in all directions, with no discernible slope. The land is so flat in this part of the country that rivers hardly flow at all, inching along, black and soil-laden.

Nevertheless, this line that divides the waters had immense effects at the end of the last Ice Age. When the glaciers began to melt, they extended nearly to present-day Iowa, nearly two miles thick in places. As they melted, the water flowed away into rivers—until the ice sheet retreated beyond the north/south divide. At that point the ice sheet itself blocked the flow of water, and a huge, shallow lake formed under the ice wall, a lake that over the centuries planed its bottom to the perfect flatness of the land today. This lake, known today by the imprint of its shorelines on the land, eventually covered part of North Dakota and much of northern Minnesota, stretching into Ontario and Manitoba. Lake of the Woods and Lake Winnipeg, both huge lakes by modern standards, are tiny remnants of Lake Agassiz, 700 miles long at its greatest extent, 110,000 square miles of ice water glittering underneath the Laurentide Ice Sheet.

This was a lake that in surface area was nearly the size of the Caspian Sea, the size of Lake Superior and Lake Huron added together and then doubled. I imagine that huge, cold water absolutely still on calm nights, or lashed by ferocious glacial winds, glistening and rocking while the great ice stands above it, so much ice that it whitens the sky and in turn glows bluely, and echoes in the dark with the trumpeting calls of great beasts.

As I picked up rocks dropped by the glacier, this spreading, extinct lake was often on my mind. But it wasn't until my late teen years, when I discovered the role of the Minnesota River in the glacial story, that I felt the full extent of the story's wonder. The Minnesota River is a small river, perhaps fifty yards wide, silt-laden, flowing slowly through southern Minnesota, curling upward to join the Mississippi at Minneapolis. The only curious thing about the Minnesota River is that it flows through a valley much too deep and wide for the river itself. When you approach the Minnesota River by car, you drive across flat fields and then suddenly come to a bluff and shoot downward into hardwood forest, into a valley as much as two miles wide.

Most prairie rivers the size of the Minnesota—the Des Moines, the Big Sioux, the Cedar, the Elkhorn— have almost no valley, but flow between their banks as if in ditches. The difference between these rivers and the Minnesota is the Minnesota's glacial ancestry. It didn't create that valley; its precursor, the River Warren, did.

As Lake Agassiz formed and spread, blocked by the Laurentide from its natural northern outlet, the ice melting at a fantastic pace, it spread over the north/

south divide and channeled itself south, through the present-day Minnesota River valley, to the Mississippi and the Gulf of Mexico.

The name geologists have given this ancient glacial drainage is the River Warren, and it was a river that deserves the name reversal: not merely the Warren River, but the River Warren. The River Warren was nothing less than one of the largest rivers that ever flowed on earth, dwarfing the Amazon, a churning, booming, iceberg-laden, miles-wide movement of water thrashing down to the Gulf of Mexico, flowing for thousands of years as the ice sheet melted.

The mild Minnesota River, meandering in its lovely valley, has a raging glacial grandparent. It wasn't until I had hunted deer and catfished for years in the Minnesota River valley that I discovered its ancestry, discovered not just the geology and science but also the myth and mystery of the place, and learned to look up at the bluff rising over me a mile away, to imagine all that air filled with moving water and to realize that I stood at the bottom of an old and immensely powerful river, the ghost of a vaster time flowing over me, through me, surging and pulsing like a drum and echo.

I've been formed by glacier, body and mind, formed by a land molded through the freezing and thawing of water. I've rafted, as a child, on a lake formed of ice-melt, waving to my father as I pushed away from him under a gray, isolating sky. Small winter, great winter. I have muscles in my legs and shoulders that formed in response to picking up glacial rocks, and my imagination has exercised itself upon the thought of ice lying deep on the land.

We are formed by our surroundings, and our surroundings contain stories that, if we learn them, form us too. The landscape of the northern prairie, which seems so passive, changeless, and lacking in surprise, is in fact a place of power and mystery to those who know its story and who carry that story on, a core of coolness in their hearts as they stoop in the sun to a rock, lift it off the earth and hold it, smelling a strange, musty scent deeper than earth, as the sky revolves above them, and from the north a cool wind springs.

Rafting

In spring, the cattle yards turned to swamps, the cattle pulling their hooves out of the mud with loud, sucking sounds. If we worked in the feedlots we buckled our overshoes tightly or we'd lose them. When we were very young, we spent hours digging channels from one large puddle in the driveway or field road to another, draining the water, watching it flow. We made miniature rivers between miniature lakes, imitating the immense and ancient history of the land without knowing it.

One April the rains came too hard and soon, and the weather warmed too fast, softening the air but not the ground, keeping the drainage tiles frozen. The constant, warm rain melted the snow that remained, and all of it lay on the frozen land. The culvert under the driveway sucked a whirlpool out of the pond that had grown there, and spewed foam violently into the pond on the other side.

The thirty-acre field behind the grove and pasture turned into a lake. I walked out in the rain one day, across the frozen, wet lawn and into the barren grove—leafless, sodden, hushed—through falling rain, and on the other side of the grove I saw it. Our world had changed. I was young, and the water spread out beyond the pasture like a sea, pocked with rain, gray as arctic ice, with faraway, black, furrowed shores.

I disconnected the electric fence at the gate between pasture and grove, climbed over the gate and reconnected the fence. The lake started in the middle of the pasture, surprising me the way it lay hidden down among the withered, winter grass. I found it first with my feet, heard myself splashing in it before I knew it was there. Then the grass faded slowly away, disappearing under the opaque march of the flood. I stood in awe and wonder, in falling rain, in rising water, in fading winter, staring at a distant shoreline over a new and reborn water.

Dad chafed. He could do no work. Finally giving in to the weather and the land, he saw promise in the water that his children only felt as unexplained yearning. We didn't know what we wanted.

He measured an old piece of plywood. He brought some iron rods from the scrap heap behind the straw stack at the east corner of the grove. He cut the rods, then brought four fifty-gallon oil drums from behind the toolshed. He pulled the old yellow welder out of the toolshed, laid rods on barrels, connected the ground clamp, stuck the welding helmet on his head, and flipped the switch. A low hum filled the air. He located the spot, flipped the visor down.

We looked away.

The arc struck, spat. Blue light played off the white shakes of the house.

The plywood fit on the rods, between the oil barrels. We found poles, long two-by-twos, from the lumber pile in the grove. We loaded pontoon raft and poles into the pickup, and Dad carted us down the field road until it disappeared under water. We unloaded the raft, dragging it ten yards to the muddy, new shore.

There is a moment when something first floats, when it is released from gravity and friction. The barrels grated on the mud and gravel, and we grunted, pushing—and then everything turned easy, the raft rose on the water and bobbed there, in small waves, waiting.

Four of us climbed on. My younger brother Colin brought a fishing pole. The raft sank again, caught on the mud, with our weight. We pushed with the two-by-twos, pushed again—and as if a rope had parted, the raft floated from shore, and like that, just like that, we were yards away, and then more yards, our poles seeking and finding the soft bottom, the sunken cornfield, pushing against it. We were explorers of a world unlike anything we'd ever known, and it was so easy, we could actually reach that far shore. We waved and waved to Dad, who stood, receding, in a blue chambray shirt, smiling where we had left him, pleased with what he had done, pleased with us.

Rocks, Roots,
and Weeds

When we had free time we spent it in the haymow above the west barn or in the grove. These were places where imagination throve, places of shadow and secrecy and small unexpectancies. As an adult I visited a patch of virgin long-grass prairie in Iowa, and I saw there how imagination might thrive on the prairie, the plants too numerous for the mind to contain—bright, delicate flowers hidden among the grass, at knee level, at waist level, and finally, at eye level or above, the compass plants bending to the sun. I was astonished at the variety and complexity. In trying to capture the imagination of the original inhabitants of this land or of the first settlers, I'd always pictured the prairie as mere grasses stretching to the horizon. Standing on that virgin prairie I sensed how much of history is contained in the land, and I understood as I never had before how altering the land distances us from entering the minds and imaginations of our forebears, since we lose what they saw, and the dreams they imposed or built on that viewing.

Students of Native American art have noted that when Indian tribes—the Lakota/Dakota for instance—moved out of a woodland habitat onto the plains, their artwork changed. Woodland art tends to be composed of curving lines and animal figures, whereas plains art consists of straight lines and geometric figures. Surely this is the influence of the land on the imagination, the straight line of the prairie exerting itself. On the modern prairie, the potential for straight lines has been taken to its maximum; roads run in straight lines with an intersection every mile, crops are planted in straight lines, buildings consist of rectangles. The Lakota, a nomadic tribe following the buffalo and the seasons, actualized the prairie's potential for straight lines through travel. European civilization, based on settlement, actualized that same potential in the architecture of roads and crops.

I'm going a long way around to return to my childhood, to say, finally, that the modern prairie is not a place that fires a child's imagination or inspires play. It may inspire games—baseball played on broad fields under a summer sky—but by "play" I mean unstructured play, where the rules themselves are invented, the external environment remade in the mind, and time reshaped internally. The first time I discovered a cornfield I was thrilled; here, it seemed, was a place I could explore, a place of secrecy. I entered it with trepidation and excitement—I was very young—wondering what I might discover there and whether I would find my way back.

Within fifteen minutes, however, time had returned to its normal flow, and the boundaries of the magic world I had begun to create dissipated. The cornfield couldn't sustain them. Its nature revealed itself to me, unvarying and without mystery. Plant after plant marched up the field, knuckled roots rising from the dirt, sharp leaves cutting the brief wind, tassels nodding, dropping pollen. Nothing changed. Within a few minutes I could see the whole cornfield, and my place inside it. I lost sight of the buildings, lost sight of the telephone wires on the driveway, lost sight of everything. I was lost to sight. But I wasn't lost. The entire structure of the cornfield was apparent in my mind. I knew that if I walked back down the row—any row— I'd emerge at the building site.

Most of the modern prairie is this way. It has succumbed to efficiency and the straight line. When I grew old enough to drive I spent much of the free time I had either in the Minnesota River valley—tramping the rolling hills and woods, following the river, deer hunting, fishing for catfish at night by a fire, learning land that couldn't be entirely grasped, that was always new—or else I spent time on abandoned farmsites, where nature had reclaimed its organic order, and where hidden things could be discovered. When I was younger, though, for this kind of play my siblings and I went to the haymow or the grove.

The haymow was full of dark corners, and tunnels created between the slope of the roof and the square bales of hay stacked there. The haymow could become anything we wanted: cliffs overlooking the sea, caves, a castle to storm or defend, a gym, an obstacle course, an airport. We could imagine and re-create the haymow, run in it, climb in it, hide in it. The grove, in many ways, was even better.

We called them Burning Weeds. It's the only name I've ever known them by. They were taller than we were, with oval, saw-toothed leaves, dark green, that seared us when we brushed against them—a mild irritant that itched and stung for about an hour and then went away. It wasn't enough to keep us out of the grove. Burning weeds covered the grove, forming a solid mat of vegetation under the huge cottonwoods, the box elders, the ash, the willows.

Like the haymow, the grove was three-dimensional. We could rise into the trees and the wind that swayed them, and there we could ride, higher and higher until the tree ceased to be a firm and passive thing, rock solid in the earth, and became instead part of the air, lithe and supple as a young woman dancing, brought alive in its love for the wind. It shifted as we clung to it, delighted, rocking high over the earth, not sure ourselves where we belonged.

And then, below, sunk within the burning weeds, our own paths trampled through them, formed to our own devices, we could run, invent the world. The grove was a haven for all kinds of weeds, not only burning weeds but others: burdock with its clumps of burrs and pale green leaves that, we read in a book, could be eaten as long as the plant was first and not second growth, which was poisonous—so we tried boiling burdock and eating it and decided we didn't like it, and we tried making yellow dye for cloth from its leaves, and green dye from willow leaves, and the dyes worked, changing the color of old scraps of white cloth that we discarded when the experiment was over, having no use for anything but the experiment itself. Wild hemp, or marijuana, grew among the burning weeds, enough to get my father arrested today, and from the hollow, stiff dead stalks we made arrows for bows we fashioned from ash limbs and baler twine to hunt the rabbits that hid in the grove, and we tried to make hemp rope but never got the technique right.

I lived on a soil so rich that anything grew on it, but what was allowed to grow was strictly controlled. Weeds were the enemy, and weeds were anything that wasn't planted. Earlier I claimed that a weed is simply a plant that has lost its relationship to other plants, and so can run amok, becoming rogue and opportunistic. Dad controlled weeds with a tenacity that almost matched the tenacity of the weeds themselves, but I thank God for the grove that sheltered them. In the grove it wasn't worth the effort or expense to pull or spray the weeds, so they grew, a rainforest tangle of vegetation through which we played and upon which we invented our own world.

The grove was the place where, weed or otherwise, nature asserted its forces without hindrance from humanity, though influenced by the things humanity had done. In the grove our minds met, not a world shaped and structured by adults, with all the rules of adults implicit in that structuring, but instead a world shaped by nature, therefore pliable to discovery, suffused with the power of myth. In the grove nothing could be broken, and rules didn't apply other than the rules we decided

upon. Our imaginations formed as we made up the
worlds that the place allowed us to invent.

Underneath the trees, underneath even the weeds, was
the Hole. In the end it was only a hole, for imagination
must always, ultimately, deal with the world as it is, and
the earth, in spite of our dreams, is laced with rock,
thickened with root. With shovels in hand, we passed
the rocks piled next to the hole in the pasture fence,
rocks dumped year after year off the bale racks until they
formed a hillock of stone. We had watched Dad blow up
some of them, driving into town in the '59 Chevy pickup and returning with thick sticks of dynamite, and we
dug down and found the rock buried long ago and
probed its bulge with our shovels. Then Dad made us
go and stand behind the pickup, and pretty soon he
came running around the fender in his work boots and
straw hat, and we clapped our hands over our ears.

That should have told us something, that dynamite. It should have told us something of the way earth
resists our efforts, how it can be stubborn as stone or
patient as a root thickening year by lightless year. But
we passed the rock pile without reflecting, passed too
the willow with drooping branches that formed a living
cave with light that moved in the wind. We walked
through the burning weeds, holding our hands high to
avoid their sting, to the section of the grove where the
ash trees grew. I had the long-handled spade, Joel the
potato fork, Colin the spade with the broken handle.

Our plan to was to dig a system of tunnels connecting this point under the ashes with all other points on
the farm—the corncrib behind the house, the east

barn, the west barn, the granary, the chicken house. We planned to dig the tunnels deep and tall and then disappear into them at odd moments—when our parents were angry with us or when our city cousins were playing tag. We would simply escape their eyes for a moment, and presto! we'd be gone, vanished into the earth like gophers. We imagined popping up to listen to the confusion our vanishing would cause, the fun we'd have out of it.

First the weeds. We swung the shovels in looping arcs, and the weeds shivered at the impact, their juices staining the metal. They whiplashed and fell, and we disentangled the shovels and swung again and again until we stood in a hollow space ten feet in diameter, a disaster of weeds at our feet, the survivors forming a wall around us.

We paused in our effort. The wind moved overhead. From the pasture we heard the thump and swish of cattle taking their singular paths. We kicked at the fallen weeds, clearing them away, then started to dig. We envisioned a narrow hole, going straight down for about ten feet, then turning sideways and heading for the corncrib. We knew it would be slow, but we had a whole summer before us, and it was only a matter of removing dirt shovelful by steady shovelful. It was only a matter of time.

Not even much time. The soft topsoil, loamy and moist, came up in large, breaking pieces, crumbling and dripping off the spades. We went straight down, kicking the shovels into the earth, hearing that strange grating that metal makes when it is forced into soil, clay parting from itself.

Two feet down we hit our first root—a new sound. I kicked the shovel in again, but it wouldn't go, so I leaned down and scraped the dirt away. There it was, a root dark and twisting and humped like a whale, disappearing at both ends into the clotted soil. I knew we'd never cut through it; my kicking of the spade had barely grazed it.

We dug the hole wider to go around the root, and made some progress again. But another foot and I felt through the sole of my boot the slick screech of metal on rock. Too big. We went around it. The pile of dirt to the side grew taller, but the hole merely flattened out, getting broader but no deeper, growing beyond our control in its own earthy way. The ground had more time than we did. The roots had been growing since before we were born, and the rocks had outlasted the glacier that had ground them in and down. It was getting to be late afternoon, and our system of tunnels was a hole about three feet deep and five feet round, and the corncrib seemed like a long ways away through the ground.

We saw a way of salvaging our work, a change of plans in response to reality. We made our way back through the weeds, over the rocks, through the pasture, through the hole into the other part of the grove, and finally to the west barn where some old corrugated metal was rusting. We dug it out of its cobwebs and dragged several pieces back to the grove, leaving a pathway of broken weeds broad as a county road behind us. We flopped the roofing over the hole and threw dirt on top of it until the metal bowed with the weight. We scattered the rest of the dirt and then, through a small opening we had left, crawled into the hole.

It was cool and close. We lay there, hidden, feeling how secret all this was, talking low, feeling the compact dirt all around us. Then we heard Mom call. We crawled back out and went in for supper.

Gradually, however, the secrecy and mystery of the hole changed. I began to realize, as the weeks went by that summer, that there was nothing to do in the hole but lie still and smell the mold and humus. I could hide, but I couldn't be free. We'd envisioned tunnels where we hid from the eyes and rules of the world, where we were suspended in the earth and could disappear and reappear as if through thin air. But we had a hole in the ground instead, with tree roots and rocks jabbing at our backs, forcing us up into air alive with the smell of weed juices and cattle.

After a month or so, I saw that the hole wasn't even a good hiding place. With the weeds knocked down around it, and the bare scar of earth, it was the most visible thing in the grove. Still, after all that work we hated to desert it. We forced it to serve as ship and fort and airplane, though we could do nothing in it but lie still, cramped together, and make noises of sirens and engines until we grew so stiff we had to leave.

Then one day I was down there alone in the darkness, among the rocks and spreading roots, when I saw a spider, shiny black, with a bloated abdomen. I could barely make it out in the small light that slanted down through the opening, but I watched it struggle up the side of the hole, its eight hairy legs groping on the clay, sending small particles of dirt rolling down into the bottom. I became acutely aware, suddenly, of how far the corrugated metal bowed into the hole from the weight of the dirt we had piled on it, how close it pressed to me. I watched the spider a moment more, moving upward, but not toward the light. An involuntary shudder passed through me that I shared this hole with that small dark thing. I crawled back out to the wind, to the light and open sky, and I never went back down.

The weeds came back. In a year, voracious as ever, they covered the fresh dirt and truly hid the place. But I always knew where it was and walked around it, for fear that if I stepped there the metal might collapse, and I would sink again to a dark place.

How Joel and I Almost
Became Mountain Men

We found the plans in a book—a way to trap a rabbit. The book was the same one that told us we could eat burdock, and the device it showed us this time was a beaut, ingenious in its simplicity, marvelous in its design. The moment I saw it I recognized its inherent goodness, and I ached, as only an eleven-year-old can, to realize that I could have thought of it myself.

Following directions, Joel and I got a wooden peach crate, discarded from Mom's canning. We took the crate back to the grove and with a saw cut a twig to the proper length, checking out the proportions in the book's picture. When we were sure we had the twig right, we propped one end of the crate up with it—and had a rabbit trap.

We stood back to admire it.

There it was, set and ready. How innocent it looked. But woe betide any rabbit who walked into it. I knelt beside the trap to see if it worked as well as the book said. I pushed against the stick, then pushed harder. The crate suddenly fell down on my wrist. If my hand had been a rabbit it would now be a trapped rabbit. I wiggled my fingers like ears and peered through the cracks of the crate. Then Joel had to try. Then I had to try again. We trapped our hands a half-dozen times. We gloated, congratulating each other, and told stories about the trophy rabbit right now wandering in the grove, fated to fall into our trap.

How could he avoid it? The trap was a marvel, and we had set it up next to the large cottonwood that lay on the way to the pasture gate. The cottonwood was one of our favorite trees. We tried to build a treehouse in it once, but the bark was too thick and corrugated for even sixteen-penny nails, taken from the bin in the toolshed, to guarantee a grip on the cambium, so we never even finished the ladder, to say nothing of the treehouse itself. This failure only increased our fondness for the tree, as something mighty, to dream of eventually climbing. Of course, when we finally grew old and skilled enough to climb the tree and build a treehouse, we no longer cared to.

We sensed that rabbits might have a fondness for this tree too, and it was only natural that at night they would come here. The book had suggested we find a "rabbit run," but we didn't know what one looked like. The cottonwood seemed as good, or better, and we were pretty proud of our placement of the trap.

But as we talked and schemed and praised ourselves for our cunning, our rabbit began to grow in intelligence. Hiding in the weeds somewhere, his brain was enlarging. From being a rather senseless animal who would *want* to bump the stick, or at least do it clumsily and accidentally, our rabbit became observant and gained a memory. Looking at the trap, he would say: "That wasn't there yesterday. Why's it here today?"

This rabbit needed persuasion. We went to the nearest corncrib—though the book didn't tell us to—and returned with an ear of corn, shelled it, and placed the kernels in a long line that led right to the trap. All the rabbit had to do now was get close, and he'd follow his stomach right in. Behind the stick we placed an entire handful of corn, a veritable jackpot that would make the rabbit throw caution to the wind and leap toward the trap, having found riches here in this ordinary place where no rabbit had ever found riches before.

We were effusive in our self-congratulations. But a few minutes later the rabbit notched his IQ up several points, keeping pace with us. We'd sprinkled the corn in a straight line. The rabbit would notice that, think that there was something peculiar and *human* about corn laid out that way. We pushed the corn about a bit, making it into a wavy, irregular line, much more natural—both we and the rabbit ignoring the larger problem that corn doesn't normally fall from the sky, in wavy lines or straight.

We couldn't believe ourselves. Wily as the rabbit was, we were always one jump ahead of him. We stared at each other and shook our heads in admiration. We'd go even further. We looked at the layout of the trap again to see what else we could do. Sheer genius led to our next move—we picked up some of the kernels we had scattered.

We nearly rubbed our hands and cackled at this depravity of insight into rabbit psychology. Now we had only hors d'oeuvres outside the trap, just enough to stimulate rabbit gluttony, and make him rush, all sense cast aside, straight at the corn piled under the peach crate.

Our prey had by now turned into a sort of rabbit-Einstein, a formidable intellectual foe who could assess the gravitational implications of pushing on a stick that supported a leaning peach crate. But this limiting of resources would blind him; crazed with greed, he would never stop to notice the stick, to say nothing of thinking about it. He'd hit it full-tilt and head-on.

Slowly the larger implications of what we'd done sank into us. We were home free, the world ours for the taking. Nature was an open hand to us, full of good things, and we could go anywhere in it, and survive on our wits alone. We were on our way to becoming mountain men, free spirits in the wilderness, surviving off the land. With this rabbit trap—and other things we'd surely invent—we could go into the deepest wilderness and find lunch.

We returned to the house with these thoughts. That night we went to bed feeling the kind of excitement usually reserved for Christmas Eve, and the guilty satisfaction reserved for a successful lie—which, to the rabbit, the trap was. I had a hard time sleeping, and when I did sleep I dreamed of dark woods under a moon, and of a pale rabbit barely visible in the trees, watching a leaning box, which cast an angular shadow in a clearing.

Nevertheless, when Joel and I did chores in the

morning we prepared ourselves for disappointment. Probably no rabbit had gone near the cottonwood during the night, we said. Probably no rabbit would be dumb enough to walk under the box and trip the stick. Any rabbit dumb enough to do that would also be dumb enough to find the trail of corn and follow it away from the jackpot. We'd never thought of that. Could rabbits be that stupid? We should have put the corn in a circle so that both ends led to the trap.

Talking this way to each other as we shoveled corn and carried it to the cattle, we convinced ourselves we'd find the trap empty. This allowed us to go to the trap with high hopes, since we'd prepaid our dues to the gods of disappointment.

We could see the trap from near the chicken feed shed, which stood just outside the grove. Our breath caught in our throats. The peach crate lay on the ground.

"It fell," Joel said.

"Maybe it was just the wind"—the wise, practical older brother.

"Yeah. Probably it was just the wind."

Then the peach crate shuffled an inch one way. Then the other.

"Did you see that?"

"It moved."

We stared at each other.

As we entered the shadow of the trees, the spirits of Daniel Boone, Jim Bridger, and Kit Carson welcomed us into the fraternity of freedom. Yesterday we'd been mere farm boys with chores to do and school to attend, but today we could take off into the wilderness and live adventurous lives, full of challenge and desperation. There before us lay the proof.

The trap moved again, frantically, shuffling along the ground but going nowhere. It dawned on us both at once that the book hadn't told us how to get the rabbit out of the trap, and it was clear from the way the box was moving that our rabbit was fierce in its struggle to escape.

"How're we going to get it out?" Joel asked.

"Maybe we could lift the box up a little and reach in and grab it."

Joel didn't reply. We both knew it was a pathetic idea. Human beings have an instinctive aversion to putting their hands into small, dark places where the hand, alone, must do its own exploring. Even an ordinary rabbit, to say nothing of this rabbit, was more than a match for a blind hand groping foolishly toward it.

While I was recovering my composure, as a mountain man having said such a ridiculous thing, and trying to think of some wise, redeeming idea, Joel took a closer look at the crate.

"It's a white rabbit," he said.

We were only a few yards away now, and sure enough, when I looked at the crate, through the slats I saw a flash of white. A white rabbit! It was astounding, magical. We'd never seen anything but plain brown cottontails in the grove. We knew that jackrabbits turned white in winter, but this was the middle of summer, and a jackrabbit was far too big to be trapped under that crate. Something truly extraordinary had happened here.

We leaned over the crate and peered into the cracks

as if we were approaching an altar to a god whose nature we didn't know, dreadful or benevolent. We stared, afraid to touch the crate, afraid to even get too close to it. Through the cracks, in the shadow, a white animal moved, its body pressed against the slats, filling the space.

"It's a chicken," Joel said.

It *was* a chicken—a dumb, idiotic, ordinary chicken. We lifted the crate. The chicken stayed hunched down, unable to believe that the fallen sky had returned to its normal distance. I shoved it with my toe.

"Get out of here. Stupid chicken."

It had eaten the corn leading into the trap but had been too frightened to eat anything inside. The corn under the crate was scattered and scratched into the ground. Prodded by my toe, the chicken stood, blinked, looked around, and then strutted stiffly away. We watched it go, forgetting that it was supposed to be inside the chicken house, doing its duty, laying eggs, not outside freeloading. We should have caught it and carried it back inside, but we didn't think of that.

"Stupid chicken," Joel repeated, as it disappeared into a thick stand of burning weed, carrying our dreams of adventure with it on its sloping back.

"Stupid trap."

"Stupid book."

Night Grove

Joel and I snuck the sleeping bags out of the attic by our parents' bedroom. We hid them in the haymow, in a tunnel between some straw bales and the roof. We'd planned for weeks. Why we thought we had to be secret about it, I'm not sure. If we'd asked our parents, they'd have certainly said yes. But we didn't want to ask them. The secret was as important as the deed, part of the adventure, part of the daring.

We went to bed dutifully and pretended to sleep, but lay there awake, listening to our parents go to bed and the house go silent in the muffled hush of eleven people breathing. Still we waited. Finally, sure that everyone was asleep, we whispered to each other, crept out of bed, and found our clothes in the dark.

We had every contingency planned. The stairway to the downstairs creaked, and its top opening was right by Mom and Dad's bedroom. But it was an old-style house with an open stairway, and a railing surrounding it at the hallway on top. We'd practiced crawling over the railing, holding on with both hands, and dropping lightly in the dark onto the bottom step, right at the living room door. First I did it, then Joel. Nobody stirred.

In the back room we put our shoes on and eased out the door into the summer night. We began to whisper, hardly able to restrain ourselves. We'd done it. We were out. No one knew. Alone, in the night, under the wide stars, and no one knew. We crept around the front of the house and made for the barn.

We retrieved the sleeping bags, so cleverly hidden, and carried them to the toolshed, which contained our other marvelous secret—two metal bars with scraps of cloth wound tightly around them at the top. We'd experimented beforehand, when Dad wasn't around, to find the right mixture of gasoline, diesel fuel, and used motor oil that, when lit, would burn brightly, but with a sustained flame. The rags were presoaked with our mixture. We carried them out of the shed and struck matches. Our torches leaped into smoky orange fire.

We set out for the grove. We'd trampled the pathways so often we didn't need light to find them, but we didn't carry the torches for their light. We carried them for the wonder of carrying them. In their shadowy, wavering light we disconnected the electric fence at the pasture, climbed the gate, and reconnected the wire. We walked through the pasture. Stars. Air. Crickets. Frogs. Silent, suspiring fields. Us. The leaping light of our torches.

At the far end of the pasture we crept through a hole in the fence back into the grove. We were at the rock pile, the small mountain of glacial rocks dug out of the land and thrown here every year—a favorite place. Joel stuck his torch into a crack between two rocks. I held mine into the pile of wood we had arranged in a circle of stone, until flames crackled. Then I stuck my torch in the rocks too, and we crawled into the sleeping bags and talked, fire before us, fire above, and the night all around—alone in it, with no one, no one at all, no one in the whole wide world, knowing where we were. The grove moved above us, dark against the stars. Tall grass brushed our faces.

We fell asleep, woke. The fire had gone out, the torches burned to charred rags. The moon rode, a half-disc, in the sky. By its light we rolled the sleeping bags, ripped the rags off the torches, and threaded our way back through the wide pasture, under all the stars wheeling in the wide, new dark. We groped for the electric fence, climbed over the gate, walked with hushed footsteps through the weeds of the grove. We replaced the bars in the toolshed and climbed the haymow to hide the sleeping bags again.

Jubilant and exhausted, we approached the house. Sarge was sleeping, his back to us, on the lawn. We crept toward him, wondering if we could fool even the dog. When we were three feet from him he woke, instantly and completely. He spun, barking, growling, an incredible wild thing, ready to tear apart whatever had frightened him.

"Sarge! It's us! It's just us!" we whispered frantically, waving our hands at him.

As instantly as he'd become wild he turned tame, wagging his tail so hard his back feet slipped sideways on the grass. We petted him, then crept back into the house, risking the steps. No one woke, and we fell asleep in our beds and were awakened in the ordinary domestic way for morning chores. All day we were tired but gleeful, the memory of the night, the secret night, our night, alone, delighting and thrilling us.

When no one was watching, we snuck the sleeping bags out of the haymow and, like a couple of criminals, by fits and starts of watching and moving, got them first to the back room, then in a quick burst through the hallway, kitchen, and living room, and upstairs to the attic. We opened the door, crawled in, and replaced the sleeping bags in the exact spot where we'd found them.

Two weeks later Mom pulled them out for some reason and wondered how they'd gotten straw in them. She asked us if we knew how that had happened, but we didn't know. We sure didn't know. What a mystery.

Dragline

A mile from our place, a dredge ditch ran alongside the county road. Because of some weirdness in the postal system routes, our mailbox wasn't at the end of our driveway but was up where the county road "T'd," near the ditch. One of our favorite things to do in the summer was to walk or ride our bikes to get the mail. Always we spent time in the ditch.

Early explorers to southern Minnesota describe it as a summer paradise. It was all wetlands, shallow lakes, and marshes teeming with ducks and geese, herons and egrets, deer, coyote, wolf, wildlife so abundant it astonished even men accustomed to wilderness. When settlers arrived on the land, they realized that the long wetland grasses formed wonderful farming soils—where they were dry. For a long time farmers farmed around sloughs, and almost every farm had one—a low-lying patch of land that contained water year-round and was surrounded by cattails and marsh grass, home to migrating waterfowl that descended from the skies in the spring and fall, establishing the land's ancient claim to wilderness.

Then in the first half of this century a massive drainage project was begun. Dredge ditches were carved out of the land. Twenty to thirty feet deep, funnel-shaped, perhaps forty feet wide at the top and tapering to about four feet at the bottom, these ditches meandered through the marsh country, sometimes following roads, sometimes angling across property. The one near our mailbox angled across Tubby Irlbeck's land, went under a bridge, turned left, followed the county road for a half mile, turned right to follow another county road, turned under another bridge, and found its way, by a series of straight lines and abrupt turns unlike anything in nature, to the Wabasha Creek, which drained into the Minnesota River.

With the dredge ditches dug, farmers could invest in tile. Our farm lay quite low, and my father saw the benefit of tile early. Eight-inch concrete tiles were laid about six feet under the land, connecting to tile laid under other farms, all of it emerging eventually in the slope of the dredge ditches. In the middle of the sloughs, "intakes" were installed—vertical tiles with metal bars over the openings to prevent cornstalks from clogging them. With these tiles in place, the sloughs were drained and land could be plowed and planted.

The scale of this drainage project boggles the mind—immense, yet mostly invisible. The dredge ditches are innocuous, hardly noticeable from a car, and one would never guess, driving mile after mile of southern Minnesota highway, that all the land is inter-laced with tile, that entire shallow lakes have been drained, and thousands of acres of swamp, to produce the endless green fields of summer.

I grew up when most of this had already taken place. A few farmers still had sloughs when I was young, but by the time I graduated from high school even our neighbor's huge slough, where the geese landed every fall, had been drained, and a wildness had gone from the land. Badgers were coming to hydrants to drink, and the geese were "V's" etched in the sky, not landing, calling overhead.

The dredge ditches themselves, however, source of the land's domestication, also became small concentra-tions of wildness. Wildness finds itself where it will, and will gladly take over what human beings have wrought. The dredge ditch was an endless source of wonder for my siblings and me. We dropped our bikes at the mail-box and, bracing our legs, descended the steep slope of the ditch to the water below. The ditches were far too deep to be mowed like road ditches, so the grass grew long and luxuriant, full of insects and scattered with wildflowers, which in a field would have been weeds.

Under the bridge just north of our mailbox, pi-geons roosted, cooing like spirits, and if we jumped on the bridge or dropped stones in the water below, they fanned out against the sky, blossoming into wings. Pheasants scurried through the long ditch grass. Fox and badger holes could be found. Frogs constantly sang and surprised us, leaping away from our feet, plunking into the water, turning instantly to smooth gold-green torpedoes. Snakes slithered in the grass. We carried one all the way home once to show our parents, horrifying Mom and amusing Dad.

There were turtles, too, though they were hard to find. Once we discovered one walking around a corn-crib, and the mystery of its slow journey, trudging across the fields, this far from water, occupied our minds for days. We carried it back to the dredge ditch, its legs and head withdrawn the entire trip, and threw it into the water, watching it drift away, so shy that even underwater it stayed withdrawn, floating volitionless, like an armored saucer tipping and drifting, until it dis-appeared. We hoped we'd done the right thing, not knowing whether it had intentions in coming to the farm or not, but assuming it'd gotten lost.

Though we never found large fish in the shallow water, minnows abounded in silvery schools. Catching them became, for one summer, an obsession. We first went splashing clumsily after them, succeeding only in fragmenting them. If we waited, they gathered again, drawn to each other by some minnow-gravity, but they darted away again at movement. We learned patience, held our cupped hands underwater for long minutes, still as the great blue herons we sometimes saw bundle into the air, alarmed from their silence, when we arrived for the mail. When the minnows swam over our hands we lifted, but were never fast enough, or they flowed away with the excess water.

Finally we applied our minds to the problem and came up with the burlap bag. Standing one on each side of the stream, our bare feet sunk into the mud, holding the four corners of the sack, we pushed it down until it was waterlogged. Then we waited, the sack underwater, watching the minnows drift near, drift away, drift near—until finally the school swam over the bag. Then we heaved and minnows flopped, full of light, on the burlap. Quickly we picked them up and placed them in quart glass canning jars borrowed from the basement and carried them home, thinking to keep them. They always died, and finally, realizing they were going to go on dying, we quit trying to capture them.

In the winter the dredge ditch froze. Though much of the ice bubbled and cracked, a few smooth, wide spots could always be found. We walked the gravel roads, in the bitter wind, carrying our skates, our faces wrapped with scarves, and descended to the lovely calm of the ditch, put on our skates, and chased each other over the ice. I dreamed of a year when the ditch would freeze perfectly, forming a smooth, glass road all the way to the Wabasha Creek, even the river, so we could skate the whole way, going somewhere, not just turning circles. It never happened, but the dream was good.

One winter I fell hard, didn't get my hands down, and landed full on my jaw on the ice, splitting it wide open. Bleeding and crying the whole way, I walked the mile home, my brothers and sisters beside me. I needed stitches, and I still have under my jaw an almost invisible scar.

Then one summer someone decided, like an impersonal force, not even a mind, that the ditch needed re-dredging. I still don't understand that decision. The tiles emptying into the ditch were at least fifteen feet or more above the surface of the water. How much silt would have to accumulate in the ditch before it lost its ability to drain the land? Could a *person* have made this decision?

All we knew was that a dragline appeared. We thought nothing of it at first. In fact, we were interested in it, marveling at its workings, its huge mouth and swinging beam. We noted its progress every time we went to town, as it worked its way down the ditch from the highway three miles north of our place, leaving mountains of mud pulled from the ditch ranging along the top.

It never occurred to us what the dragline was doing to the ditch. Over the weeks of that summer it continued south until it stood at the curve into Tubby Irlbeck's land, and then at the bridge over the road, then across from our mailbox, then on down the road. Only after it had passed did we realize the devastation. It left a wasteland. It left nothing. It took everything and left nothing. It turned the ditch into just that—a ditch, a scar in the ground with muddy water at the bottom in which nothing stirred.

The minnows never returned. The frogs disappeared. The herons gave up. Still, we hoped. The next summer we checked, thinking that the animals would return. Nothing. Nor the next summer. Getting the mail became just getting the mail. I hated, finally, to even descend the ditch, to see the nothing that was there.

I was just old enough, around twelve or thirteen when this happened, to know what loss was, and to question its necessity. I understood what I'd lost, and it was like something cut away from my childhood, excised from my heart. Even now, as an adult, I'm sometimes surprised to find myself angry about it. It wasn't until I was old enough to drive, and discovered the Minnesota River valley, and learned to tramp its hills, learned to stay out all night around a campfire fishing for catfish, the big water going by in the moon, that I found again a place that contained the same kind of wonder and mystery that the dredge ditch had.

The Eye,
Taken to Eternity

Erazim Kohak, in *The Embers and the Stars,* says that human beings exist in time and eternity both. We make our lives within the hour-by-hour and the day-to-day, but we sense—and more than sense, know—the eternal. Much of life on a farm, like life anywhere else, consists of overwhelming hours—time inexorably passing and jobs that must be done. But when you live upon the land, even if that land has been domesticated for farming, there are times when hours disappear, when your activities are ruptured by the disturbing grace of other beings who take you out of your limited world, to the pure moments where, as Kohak claims, eternity resides.

One's world during fieldwork is normally constrained by the front end of a tractor, five or six feet away, and the back end of an implement, ten feet away. It is a moving world; you carry it with you as you go up and down the rounds, but you remain at its center, and

its perimeter doesn't change. I much preferred the bod-
ily involvement of feeding cattle. Fieldwork bored
me—sitting, watching, while the tractor did all the
work. But sometimes my eye would leap beyond its
constraints, drawn outward by something stronger than
boredom or my will.

It could happen in the simplest way. Sitting on the
Five-Sixty, ear muffs on to block the noise, pulling a
disc behind me across cornstalks, with the dust I raised
sweeping over me in a trailing wind, I'd suddenly see
the earth itself leap up, and my eye would jerk away
from the front wheel. Suddenly distance would startle
me, marked by the rising white tail of a jackrabbit
bounding over the broken stalks, as if the jack could
take the air any time it chose. Before my eye adjusted, in
that split second before depth perception made sense of
the world, the rabbit could be as large as a deer, leaping
over the featureless field. And when my eye did adjust,
distance opened up behind the rabbit as I followed it
out of sight, finding again the world I had lost to work
and hours.

Herons might fly over, trailing legs, their necks
crooked over their backs, spooky in their largeness,
never flying high. In the moment before I recognized a
heron, my heart sensed something far more ancient,
pumped violent blood into my veins, the shadow of
some ancient mammalian fear of flying reptiles, ptero-
dactyl wings, cast into my body from immemorial time.

Small creatures, too, could draw me out into a
world larger than myself, a world interrelated and complex. Robert Burns, in his poem "To a Mouse"—which,
when I first encountered it in college, I memorized, so

strongly did I feel it—recognized the emotional power of mice, so busy, small, and helpless. Like Burns, I saw them most often while plowing.

A moldboard plow cuts into the ground ten inches to a foot deep, lifts the soil, and turns it over. If the coulter in front of the share is working properly, it acts like a giant pizza slicer, rolling through the soil and cutting an edge abrupt and perpendicular. When you plow, you run the right rear wheel of the tractor in this furrow. Every once in a while a field mouse, fleeing the tractor, would make the mistake of descending into the furrow. For a mouse, the bottom of the furrow, neatly planed by the plow, is like a highway, but the mouse has no idea that the furrow is the one place it doesn't want to be.

Plowing is slow, but a field mouse is slower. I'd see the mouse ahead of me, scuttering along, the furrow wall like a cliff to its left, unassailable, and to its right the ragged, plowed land, full of humps and holes, onto which, terrified, it would never venture, needing all its speed. The Five-Sixty and the Super M were both row crop tractors, with narrow front ends, so the front wheel didn't ride in the furrow. First the front end of the tractor would gain on the struggling mouse, then pass it—tiny thing down there, not much slower than the tractor—the tractor just faster, but inexorably faster. Front wheels, fan, muffler, cylinder block—slowly the tractor moved its roaring bulk past the small creature, and the huge, lugged wheel rose over it.

It was a strange sensation, and not a pleasing one, to find myself so much more powerful than another creature. There was no ambiguity in, no sugary veil to be cast over, the relationship I had with the mice that ran down the furrow, as the rear wheel of the tractor rose over them. They were small and helpless, I was huge and powerful, and nothing in their instincts could take them from the furrow.

I could never run the mice over. Boredom led me to a game. I'd let the rear wheel of the tractor rise over the mouse, until the mouse disappeared under the curve. Then I'd kick the clutch, the tractor would stop, and the mouse would reappear, still struggling down the furrow. I'd sit on the idling tractor, waiting for the mouse to get ahead of me, then start again, gradually, gradually gaining on the mouse, until once again it disappeared under the curve of the great, lugged tire—and I'd kick the clutch again, and watch the creature reappear.

Until this grew boring too. Then I'd stop the tractor, let it idle, and sit in the fall air, the world suddenly larger than it had been, vast and incredible seen from a mouse's view, and wait until the mouse had time to use an instinct other than running and leave the furrow, creeping onto the plowed land.

Other creatures of the fields, by their sheer ferocity, taught me respect and even fear. I'd sometimes see badgers humping over the land, flat and compact, carrying their reputation for toughness on their striped backs. If we found a badger hole, we always spoke quietly around it, as if the hole were a sacred oracle containing a powerful spirit of the earth, which, I'm convinced, a badger may well be.

One night, in the year after Dad died, the dog wouldn't stop barking. He woke the whole house. I heard my four sisters murmuring in their room across the hall, my three brothers who were still at home stir-ring. The stairs creaked, and my mother's footsteps sounded softly on the kitchen floor below me. The front door opened and she shouted at Sarge. For a moment the barking stopped, then it started again. I climbed down from the bunk bed and went to the windows of our room overlooking the porch and front yard. In the summer moon I saw the dog, pale white, legs braced, barking at the pump house and hydrant near the garden.

I put on clothes and went downstairs. Mom couldn't control Sarge. He never hurt or threatened children, but he could frighten adults. There were salesmen who wouldn't get out of their cars with Sarge barking at their windows. I found Mom in the kitchen. We spoke a few quiet words, then I stepped onto the porch and tried my luck. When I shouted, Sarge looked back over his shoulder, then started in again.

I went to the back room for the .22. You never knew. He might have an animal trapped out there, and he didn't feel big enough to take it on. I didn't want my added presence to frighten it into trying to take us both. And if it did, I wanted to be prepared. I grabbed a flashlight, but it didn't work. Our flashlights never worked, batteries always dead. So I grabbed the car keys instead.

I backed the car up, swung it around, and posi-tioned it right behind Sarge. I thought I saw, in the headlights, a shadow of something near the pump house. I got out, walked to the dog, put my hand on his head to quiet him, and peered into the lights. The cor-ner of the pump house cast a shadow that made it hard to see. I didn't want to go much closer. I trusted Sarge's instincts for necessary distance. Finally I made out two animals crouched against the pump house—badgers, a large one and a small, a mother and a cub.

Sarge was smarter than I thought, not wanting to tangle with a badger. I always liked having badgers around. It was good to know they were there, good to hear stories of their toughness, good to have them living their indomitable lives on our land—except that when a badger was around, it was always the badger's land. That is part of the mystery and aura of a truly wild creature. That aura changes what you think you know of your position and place, and shatters mere human and temporal concepts like ownership—and in so doing shifts the balance of the entire world, changes everything, and gives you access to the eternal.

It was good, as I stood with Sarge in the summer night, to feel the little fear I felt, to not want to go closer, not want to provoke those claws and that dervish body. It is a fear akin to holy fear, such fear is. I watched for a while. The badgers huddled there.

Then I walked back to the car, as Sarge started barking again. I swung the car around, reparked it, leaned the gun against the fender, and found a piece of baler twine. We couldn't just pull Sarge away from things. He had his own will, and he'd resist. But he never understood a leash. I walked back to him, tied the twine around his collar, and led him into the house, to the mudroom, where we dressed in our outdoor clothes. Sarge never slept in the house, but I made an exception. I didn't know how long it would take for the badger to decide she was safe and venture with her cub away from the pump house, where her back was protected, and into the open. She was probably gone already, but I wanted to make sure.

It was a hot, dry summer. When we watered the garden the hose leaked, forming a puddle under the hydrant. They'd come for that water. The closest free water, not connected to a farmsite, was the dredge ditch a mile away. For several weeks after that we made sure the puddle remained when we went to bed, but the dog never woke us again.

But perhaps even more than badgers, hawks take the eye and mind away from the temporal world. In the eighteen years I spent on the farm, twice I saw hawks gather in the fall, riding the thermals over the warm land. Once we were doing chores, once I was alone in the fields. Both times I saw them only by accident—a glance upward, my eye catching a movement, the flash of red light off a tail feather, enough to arrest the glance and keep it there, on a single hawk wheeling in the vast dome of the sky—until, like some strange magic show, other hawks appeared, then more and more, the eye finding them as it adjusted to its seeing, as if the air were creating them, their shapes receding upward into the blue, in a high, resounding column, receding out of sight, the near ones reflecting light as they banked their wings, the far ones no more than black spots, and beyond that even, the invisible ones, only imagined up there where the earth touches space and infinity.

They cut across each other's paths, wheeling and soaring, the thermal narrow enough to contain them, so that they were like a slow and stately and beautiful

tornado of birds, directing the eye only upward, beyond its own capacity for seeing. A single hawk circling
the land, searching for a field mouse, can be, depending
on your mood, no more than an animal seeking its next
meal. But dozens of hawks riding a high column of air
direct your eye to eternity, and your eye can't help but
look.

Working

In November the calves arrived from a western ranch, packed into semis, barely weaned and wild as deer. They poured out of the metal doorway, clattered down the ramp, and took off, getting as far away from anywhere as they could. If they'd ever trusted humans, that trust had been destroyed by their recent handling—branded, castrated, hauled to a sale barn, forced into trucks, to emerge at a place they'd never seen. They lit out.

But they couldn't go far. Dad put up gates to confine them near the barn and feed bunks. After the trucks left, we stood at the fence and watched them. They watched us. Splayfooted on the concrete, knock-kneed, suspicious, they huddled against the windbreak, white-faced or black, waiting for attack, so frightened their manure ran out of them like water.

It took weeks before they settled down. Some developed shipping fever, their immunity so decreased

125

from stress they died unless treated with antibiotics. In time, corn and silage and good alfalfa hay won them over. When they came on their own to the bunks at feeding time, Dad released them to the larger cattle yard.

A trucker once commented that Dad's cattle were the tamest he'd ever worked with. That didn't surprise us. We had no automatic feeders and were constantly with them. We filled two-handled aluminum baskets with ground corn or silage and carried them down the row of bunks, the cattle's heads lined up like sentries. We'd dump a basket at the end of the last bunk, turn, start down the row of heads, pass a brother coming toward us with a full basket, fill the basket again at the feed wagon, start down the row of heads, pass a brother with an empty basket, dump the full basket not at the end of the last bunk now but two basketfuls away—and so on, until we had worked our way back to the feed wagon. The cattle got so accustomed to our feet passing by them that we sometimes tripped over their outstretched heads reaching for spilled grain, and we pulled on their ears on the return trip or played games, trying to push their heads out of the bunks while they pushed back, reserving their places.

More than anything else—more than school, than church, than crops, than family or community activities—the cattle shaped our time and informed the way we lived our daily lives. Everything else could be postponed for a while without doing irreversible harm or making a noticeable demand on us, but failing to feed the cattle resulted, within an hour, in loud bawling and bellering from the yard.

Only once in all my childhood did our family take a trip that took my father away from the cattle overnight—and this was only after Kevin was in high school, old enough to do chores alone. He stayed home, and Renee with him, because she had no interest in the trip. The rest of us piled into two cars and drove three hundred miles to Moose Lake, Minnesota, where Dad's sister and her family lived. We visited Duluth, saw a bridge that rose for tankers to go under it, saw ships hundreds of yards long, saw water we couldn't see across and so clear that the bottom was visible ten feet down—all new things to us, all amazing and magical, accustomed as we were to land, land everywhere, and water small and murky.

If we went to a lake for a Sunday of fishing in the summer, we rose early, did chores, changed clothes, went to early mass, went back home, changed clothes again, packed gear and headed out, usually to Kandiyohi Lake, fifty miles away, arriving, if things went well, with enough time for a swim in the green water before lunch. After lunch we fished for bullheads with worms and bait-casting reels and heavy, teardrop sinkers—then when we were sick of fishing, we went swimming again. By the time our second swim was over, we had to pack so we could make it home in time for afternoon chores.

When school started in the fall and classmates told of going to the ocean or the mountains on vacations, I wanted to go on vacations too—longed for vistas, for heights, for thin air, for space, trees, adventure, the possibility of getting lost. But I never expected such things and so never felt bitter or resentful toward the cattle. The classmates who took vacations were "town kids";

town kids and farm kids had different lives. Far from lording it over the farm kids with their superior freedoms, the town kids—at least the boys—were a little embarrassed by their easy lives. In fifth grade one of them read a persuasive essay in front of the class, with the impressive title: "The Work of Town Kids and Farm Kids." He argued that, though farm kids thought they worked harder, the truth was that town kids also had much to do—mow lawns, take out the garbage, help around the house—and that if all things were considered, the workloads were even.

Sister Joanice thought he did a good job of making his case, but what did she know? The consensus on the playground, where the real authority lay, was that the writer of the essay was a Retard, and that a farm kid did more in an afternoon than a town kid did in a month. What? He thought we didn't have lawns to mow? And lawns ten times as big as the postage stamp he had, with some of the yard—down past the big corncrib—composed of crabgrass you had to go over twice to get cut, the first time with the mower tilted at a forty-five-degree angle to keep it from stalling. And taking out the garbage? Did he think farm kids didn't have garbage to take out? And not just household garbage but empty feed sacks and seed sacks and supplement sacks, and oil cans and fluid cans.

And what about walking beans, pulling the weeds by hand, not to make money, like he did, but just because it had to be done? Baling hay? Pitching silage? Cutting down dead trees—with a bucksaw. What about picking rocks? What about grading the driveway—did he have to *grade* his driveway?

And framing it all, every morning and afternoon, seven days a week, what about doing chores?

What about those cattle shuffling in the dark even before you rise from bed, their expectant stomachs churning? What about their cloven hooves cutting through the soft mud of the cattle yard, leaving half-moon prints as they leave the corncob pile where they have lain since last they ate, digesting, chewing their cuds, rising once in a while to test the electric fence, returning, chewing, their front legs curled under them, their back legs too, gazing into distance and chewing, marking time by the side-to-side grind of their teeth and the heave of their cuds up from their stomachs, and the passage of darkness and the gray dawning in the east, and birdsong and the absence of bats and the re-shaping of the world into light, until they lift their empty stomachs up from the cobs and follow one another, loose-jointed, their hooves curling up from the cattle-yard earth, nose-to-tail, in the paths they have cut from the cobhill to the bunks, until they fight and find their places, shoving, butting, pushing, the strongest ones at the end where they know the corn will first be dumped, the weaker ones near the feed wagon, so that by the time we arrive, sleepy, barely out of bed, they are all watching us, 300 eyes, 150 anvilfaces, 300 ears tipped forward.

What about the cattle lining the bunks again by the time we returned from school? What about the small space we managed to carve for ourselves after walking the long driveway home from the bus, time for a sandwich and a few cookies and for reading the comics from the *New Ulm Daily Journal*, which arrived by mail a day late—"Alley Oop," "Priscilla's Pop," "L'il Abner," "Nancy"—until we had to rise and go upstairs and change into work clothes. By the time we finished chores in the winter, including bedding the cattle down with straw scattered in the barns, it was dark, and we walked under the stars to the house for supper, as we had walked out of the house under the stars that morning.

It is all so huge and powerful that it finally leaves behind the question of mere work. It *was* work, and hard work, but never did I dread rising in the morning to it, as I did when I was older, working my way through college, and had a job at a place called Trademark Homes, manufacturing modular houses. I punched a time clock and began work to a whistle, and had a boss whose head swelled up when he put his hard hat on so that he couldn't take it off even during lunch break, and who saw us all as part of his machine for turning out cheap houses.

I came to that job with immense experience in hard and independent labor, and a love for it—for sweat, for the changes the body can accomplish in the world, for the rhythms the body discovers in even the most boring tasks and the rhythms people find in each other—such intimate knowledge—when they are working together: brother passing brother down the lines of hungry heads; stepping away from the small door in the silo, having thrown my forkful of silage down the chute a half-second before Kevin's fork whizzes through the space where I'd been, he not even looking to see if I've left it, as, in a few more seconds, I'll slash my fork not

looking through the space he's emptied; crawling into
the haymow to throw down hay to Joel or Colin waiting below for it, the decision having been made between us who will do which job, no order or command
but only the mutual knowledge that each half of the job
is necessary, and if one half is harder, then tomorrow
the roles will be reversed.

To move from this, from work as self-knowledge
and world-knowledge, work as the most intimate way
to know another person—a knowledge of bone and
joint and pulse, a knowledge of another contained in
your own body, in the way it slows down or speeds up
to maintain pace—work intermixed with awe at stars, at
moon, at clouds, at how immensely cold it can get in
the winter, at the sun coming up over a flat, white, barren landscape, sometimes a pure red ball, sometimes
boiling and aflame with clouds, awe at how cattle carry
frost on their backs, at how horseflies cut loud, irides-
cent curves, seeking blood and opportunity—to move
from all this to a whistle, an assembly line, a boss who
tells you what to do and how fast to do it, is not in any
manner to move from work to work. It is to move from
lived life to prison, from responsibility to the tempta-
tion to sabotage, from expansion of body and mind to
their constriction and atrophying.

I've done the dirtiest work imaginable: cleaned barns
with a pitchfork, wading into manure accumulated
over months; cleaned under chicken roosts, the ammo-
nia released from the manure cutting at my nasal mem-
branes; shoveled oats, full of itchy dust, into a grain
auger. I grew up using my back, but never did I feel it

as indignity. I'm not saying I enjoyed it all. No one in his right mind would enjoy cleaning chicken roosts— but there's a vast difference between disliking something and feeling undignified by it.

Along with hunting and fishing when I got older, work was my strongest contact with the world. It pulled me beneath the suffocating realm of comfort and convenience where the modern world allows us to live. In so doing, work let me breathe. Every morning during my childhood and adolescence I woke up to deep and driven contact with the world: the touch of dirt, the affinity of beasts, the sting of wind, the breath of open air, the sense of the world as physical and spiritual, harsh and gracious both.

For me, experiencing the world was done as part of something necessary, part of cattle rising and moving down pathways to feed bunks, depending on me to get out of bed and face the world as it *was* that particular morning. Chores weren't called off for rain or snow or hundred-degree heat; the work drove me deep under the surface of the world, beyond comfort or complacency, to powers, dominions, principalities, dancing and intertwined.

I'm puzzled by people who divide manual work from recreation—who spend money on a riding lawn mower or snowblower and then spend even more money on a fitness center membership so they can get their exercise. I know a man who gets in his car and drives a few blocks to the track so he can jog around it. To stay in shape myself I run, three or four times a week, and play tennis. I also cut my grass with a ground-driven reel mower, shovel my driveway with a scoop shovel, till my garden with a spade, cut my own firewood to heat my house, and walk rather than drive to my job. Sometimes these jobs are boring—but the truth is that half the time I find jogging to be boring also. Lifting weights looks to me like the most incredible boredom imaginable. I don't understand those who rave about how much they love to lift weights and then won't walk a half-mile on an errand. If I'm sometimes bored by running—so-called recreation—I am sometimes refreshed by, say, shoveling snow, and I feel the old rhythms in it, the musical attunement of body to the task, and I'm glad snow fell to make this soaring movement necessary, to drag me from the house and reconnect me to my blood and breath, and to the physical world.

A major difference between work and recreation is that the first is done when the task demands it, the second at our convenience and choosing. But it is precisely because we can't choose when we do work that it can be richer than recreation. If it's raining or too cold, I may choose not to run, but since I don't have a parking sticker and therefore have to walk to work, I have to (but the truth is, I *get* to) experience all the weather the world happens to be offering in the time it takes me to go from my house to my office.

I get to walk under an umbrella. (My children love walking under umbrellas, but most adults have forgotten that particular joy, won't let themselves experience it.) If it's nice in the morning but raining in the afternoon and I don't have an umbrella, I get to be soaked through by the time I reach home. (Children love to be soaked, inventing games to accomplish it, but most

adults have forgotten that particular, joyful discomfort.)
I get to have wind cut my face, get to have snow sting it.
I get to walk through drifts up to my knees. Sometimes
I get to walk backward in the winter, the wind is so
cold, and I know for a certainty the world is there, de-
manding, foreign, other, yet utterly a part of me, I a
part of it. I get to watch the creek steam on cold days,
get to break a sweat on warm ones, get to walk in mists,
get to shiver.

The cattle were always testing the electric fence, bump-
ing up against it, getting shocked, backing away. If it
grounded out, wire alone wouldn't keep them in. Usually we'd know about a ground through the static it created on the radio, and go out and walk the fences until
we found the bad insulator or the juicy weed touching
the wire and post, and make the repair. Sometimes,
though, the cattle would go through the fence before
we knew it was grounded out. We'd discover the fence
was bad by looking out the window and finding a steer
in the front yard or garden, or a half-dozen cattle trot-
ting up the driveway. One year nearly the entire east
herd escaped after the corn had grown to full height.
They disappeared into the fields—a minor disaster, calling forth communal help. Neighbors who had horses
rode the country looking for them. We received calls
from people miles away telling us they'd seen a steer
crossing a road. We eventually got all but one of them
back, but it took almost a week, and was a major news
item, though not a printed one.

The most vivid memory I have of the cattle escap-
ing, however, is the time we discovered them out after

dark, in the middle of a thunderstorm. Most of us were in bed when our parents called us downstairs. We jumped up and scrambled into our clothes; escaped cattle, like fires, demand speedy responses. Luckily they hadn't gotten far, and only about five were out. We rushed into the cool rain, farmer caps on our heads to keep our glasses dry, thin and worthless coats on, leather boots, jeans. The wan glow of the yard light did little against the amazing darkness.

Dad had spotted one of the steers around the corner of the granary. He headed that way, calling orders like a military commander, devising strategy, positioning his men—or in this case his sons and daughters. You can't go barreling out in a herd to chase cattle—they'll simply run away from you, and the more you chase the faster and further they'll run. Instead you have to estimate how far they've gone and circle around to get in front of them, then have people positioned in the right places to turn them into the gates you've opened back into the cattle yard. It's tricky, difficult maneuvering, and very often they'll squirt through your defenses, making it necessary to improvise a new strategy on the spot.

In the lightning flashes we could see a few white faces down past the granary. The herd was composed of Angus and mixed-Angus steers. The black bodies, even in the lightning, were almost invisible, but the white heads stood out like foolish ghosts through the rain. Dad quickly positioned us. My job was to go to the big gate between the barn and the iron pile, open it wide, make sure no more cattle escaped from it, and then stand near the corner of the north corncrib so that when the escapees were chased around the granary, I could turn them toward the gate rather than have them line out toward the grove.

I lugged the gate open in complete darkness, rain pouring down, gurgling off the gutterless barn roof, streaming past the bill of my cap. The gate was heavy, made of two-by-eights. I opened it in lurches, heaving it three feet, dropping it, heaving it, the wood smooth and slick in my hands, smelling of wet cattle from the hair they'd rubbed off against the bolts. From down by the lone box elder in the southeast corner of the farm-site I heard Dad calling orders, and a "Ha!" from a brother, who was helping chase, and then a "Ha!" from a sister, who was positioned, I guessed by the sound, between the tree and big corncrib, to keep the steers from turning into the field there.

They were on their way. With a final lurch I laid the gate wide open, stepped toward the cattle yard, and yelled to frighten off any curious steers attracted by my activity. In a lightning flash I saw a few of them, sus-pended by the blue strobe, kicking their hooves in the rain-pocked yard. I left the gate and went to the corn-crib completely soaked through, the grove a blacker black swaying against the close sky.

I was pretty miserable—dragged from bed, my thin coat clinging to my skin, my hair soaked right through my cap, water squishing out of my socks with each step. I stood alone at the corncrib, listening to the shouts of my father and siblings, and to the barely audible clatter of hooves on gravel. Stupid, stupid cattle. My bed lay warm and empty, and here I was, awake and rained upon, a sentry for stupidity, a guard against these idiot, random animals.

Lightning flashed again, and out of the dark, only a few feet away, charged a lumbering chunk of nostrils and wide-eyed night—one of the pure Anguses, slick black from fetlock to forehead, the sound of its hooves softened by grass, wild with freedom and pursuit. The lightning destroyed darkness except for this one solid piece that was suddenly there, black as an eight-hundred-pound bowling ball, and I a single pin.

I was alone in the darkness when the lightning flashed, and then I wasn't alone but standing motion-less while an eight-hundred-pound steer, rain smacking off its back, barreled toward me. I raised my hands and yelled, an instinctive movement from having worked cattle so often, and as the world faded again I saw the animal's head shift slightly and knew its body would fol-low, and then in the darkness the ground whumped under its weight only a few feet away, and I smelled its wet, oily hide and felt its airwash brush my wet cheeks, and I closed in behind it to keep it moving toward the open gate.

The arrow of surprise and fear collapsed and spread into relief, and suddenly turned to joy—as it will—because I was alive. The living rain seemed wonderful and full of music, and my father's voice and the scram-ble of hooves and the smells of the night seemed won-derful, and my brothers and sisters were wonderful, bringing the cattle toward me, so well, so damned incredibly well, and I exactly where I should be to turn them toward the yard.

The discovery—as opposed to the imposition—of rhythm in work, like the discovery of rhythm else-where—in language, in music, dance, waves, the sea-sonal return of the stars, the flap and glide of a bird, the flow of sports—is a satisfaction, sometimes a deep and abiding joy. Feeding the cattle allowed the discovery of rhythm within rhythm, a polyphony so complex it takes a whole life to understand and appreciate it.

At the deepest, bass level, the longest rhythms were the stories of the land itself, and of how generations had made a living on it, of how my grandparents had arrived on it, farmed it, how my father had taken it over, how he had milked cows and then changed to beef cattle—a slow development in wavelengths of decades.

Above this, in the baritone wavelengths of years, was the annual arrival of the new, lost calves, their wari-ness and increasing familiarity, their eventual disappear-ance into another truck—a gentle, cruel, common, ex-traordinary cycle, sustaining and informing everything else.

The tenor, diurnal rhythm of chores shaped our days, the work that began before breakfast, the cattle fed before we ate, and then fed again in the middle of the afternoon in summer, or wedged against the night in winter.

Within this was the alto rhythm of working together, a rhythm refined so that brother could pass brother in the bunks without interference, so that the rusty silage fork swinging through space met only an open door and not a brother's leg. There was the roll of shoulders, the bending of legs, the entire body moving up from the ground, unfolding to send a scoop of corn through the air in a lovely, fading arc into the hammermill.

Finally, there were the autonomous, soprano rhythms of the body—blood pounding in the temples, winter breath clouding vision, the limit that the body reaches, known without thought: this can be sustained, right here, until the time comes for a break, until the hammermill is full or the cattle fed or the barn yellow with straw.

This is what remains—the memory and knowledge of a music—after the sweat has dried, the muscles relaxed, the heart quieted its pounding, and the meandering paths of the cattle covered by weeds, the shuffle of hooves receded into wind, the brothers gone to separate lives, and the farm itself passed into another cycle, as have the generations.

Slow Flies

The plywood above me was black. In the rising morning light it glittered like some dull, half-slumbering eye too dim to intend evil but evil nevertheless. I was focused on getting the cattle fed, and at first I didn't notice. I walked into the feed wagon with a scoop shovel and a two-handled basket, set the basket down, and dug into the ground corn with the shovel. It was September, the first fall morning cold enough to require both sweatshirt and coat for morning chores—not insulated coverall weather yet, but weather of visible breath.

I filled the basket, but as I leaned the shovel against the side of the wagon an eerie feeling, different from cold, slid down my spine like a string pulled. The sun had risen higher, and a ray of orange light came into the shadow of the wagon. I saw a dark iridescence above me and looked up.

Six inches from the top of my head in the low wagon flies covered the plywood, moving slowly, like withered cripples, but so thick they seemed like a plane of strange, evil water. They spread away from my eye, shifting. The near ones bumped against each other, their veined wings held tight to their fat, torpedo bodies, their legs barely moving, blind and volitionless. I stepped out of the wagon.

All summer Mom fought flies. One who hasn't raised livestock in a humid, hot climate can't imagine it. The barns teemed with them. They rose in clouds, like tendrils of rain falling upwards and sideways. We walked through them as through a dark mist. A single fly buzzes. A cloud of flies howls.

If we expected company in the summer, Mom gave several of her children the job of killing flies. It was search and destroy: first the ones in the house, stalking them with flyswatters and striking them dead, satisfying smacks and the bodies falling off the wall, crumpled and broken, wings at odd angles. There might be five, ten, fifteen, in the living room and kitchen.

When we'd accomplished our mission inside we went out to the porch, where the real work began. Flies clung to the screen, spotting the shakes. Company couldn't be expected to shoo them away before entering the house. Timing was important—if we killed them too soon, reinforcements might arrive from the barns before the company came, and if we did it too late, we might not finish sweeping them off the porch in time.

So there we'd be, perhaps three of us, glancing up the driveway for the arrival of the guests, our ears cocked for the dog's bark, smacking flies like the tailor in the fairy tale, exclaiming when we got three or four at a blow. If the guests were fairly intimate and the visit informal, we might go on smacking flies through the dog's frenzy and the car's approach down the long driveway, might even greet the guests with flyswatters in hand, and share condolences about the problem of flies, along with comments on the heat and humidity. If the visit was formal, however, and our timing bad, and the car appeared in the driveway before we finished, we had about thirty seconds to stow the flyswatters and sweep the porch, flinging the dead flies into the flower bed, where they disappeared against the black soil.

I've seen pictures of dry places in Africa where children have flies crawling about their eyes for the moisture and the children don't bother to brush them away. I hope never to become that familiar with flies, but they were part of how I grew up —annoyances mainly, no more—like the smell of cattle yards in rain, or sleeping in the same room with four brothers.

Only once, during one particularly wet summer, did Dad try to do something about the flies. Golden Malrin Fly Bait was advertised on the radio out of Redwood Falls, in words that made it sound like a scientific wonder and an avenue to paradise. Listening to the advertisement you could believe—and to some extent I did—that it would change the quality of the light, that hard things would become easy, and that happiness would become a permanent, though flexible condition.

So I was pleased when Dad finally gave Golden Malrin a try, returning from the grain elevator with a two-gallon pail of it. He wouldn't let us handle it, but allowed us to watch him, gloves on, scatter it in a wide path around the east barn, where the flies had become legion.

I was disappointed when he opened the pail. Inside were bright, synthetic-blue crystals. Why would they name it Golden Malrin, a name that rolled off the tongue like a promise, when it was fluorescent blue? It didn't look at all like the wonderful solution to life's problems that the radio advertised. I thought that Dad had managed, in the way of parents, to get the wrong thing. I checked the bucket: *Golden Malrin Fly Bait*. There was a betrayal here somewhere.

Still, I came back from cultivating corn that day eager to observe the effects of Golden Malrin. When I went to the east barn to help with chores, I found a killing field.

Mass death is astonishing and dreadful, no matter how small the individual deaths, how insignificant the bodies that have stilled. The Golden Malrin still lay in the gravel between the granary and barn, like glints of decorative stone some town person might use in landscaping, but it was covered with thousands—millions?—of dead flies. Dead flies. Black, silent, dead flies. The feed wagon lay fifty feet away, over a carpet of shriveled bodies. I went to it on tiptoe, trying not to hear the flies' bodies breaking under me in the silence of their not-buzzing.

A breeze rippled down the alleyway between the buildings and a small surf of flies rose in it, a faint black pipeline, until it broke against the shiplap siding of the barn and the flies that composed it fell out of the air, becoming a dune against the foundation. The commercials had understated Golden Malrin; I'd imagined nothing this effective. But I'd expected broad, effusive results, not this terrible focus and intent. Golden Malrin baited flies and killed them before they even had a chance to go somewhere else to die.

But even Golden Malrin couldn't tempt every fly on the farm. They returned to their usual numbers. That September morning, as I stood outside the feed wagon, I realized that cold had caught them unawares. The evening before they had convocated upside down on the feed wagon cover, and during the night the temperature had dropped to near freezing. Now light was urging them to move, but their sluggish bodies wouldn't respond.

A fly is three things—dirty, ugly, and quick—and quickness is its major irritation and redemption; if you shoo it, it will move, and fast enough that you don't see its dirtiness and ugliness. A slow fly is reduced to dirty and ugly, and above me now dirty and ugly were crawling.

From outside the feed wagon I looked at the flies teeming and massed—stupid, senseless, incoherent. I felt pitiless. I picked up the scoop shovel, turned it upside down and, staying outside the wagon, swung it upward, flat against the board.

The sound of a hundred flies dying, a victory far greater than the tailor's Seven-at-One-Blow, was lost in the bang of the board. Inside the wagon, as if in a strange, miniature, but complete landscape, a black rain rained. Over the flat plains of the feed wagon floor, over the foothills and rising mountains of ground corn, the plywood sky poured down its burden. Slow, groping bodies condensed and fell, almost weightless, through the cold. They landed on the ground corn, and their feet went slowly on the particles, moving anywhere, nowhere, congealed. They fell in a black mist, without volition. But their legs kept moving.

Frozen Silage

In Minnesota the winter cold gives no pause or relief. In order to do chores in the morning we put on our ordinary work clothes and two or three pairs of socks, then thick hooded sweatshirts and insulated coveralls, two sets of gloves, stocking caps, and boots. On really cold days we put a coat over the coveralls, though the bulkiness made work difficult.

The Oliver and the International Five-Sixty, both diesels, sometimes wouldn't start, even if plugged in, even with starting fluid. Some Saturdays we had to grind corn with the Super M, making the work in the cold that much longer, since we had to pace ourselves more slowly to keep from killing the engine. The cattle spent the nights packed into the barns on straw we spread for them, having deserted the cobhills in the yards, where the wind was always blowing.

The motor on the electric elevator, which transported silage to the feed wagon, groaned and whined when we plugged it in. Two of us waited in the feed wagon, two of us climbed the galvanized steel chute to the top of the silo, making sure to step over the elevator since it had a short in it and shocked us if we touched it. Dad always intended to fix that short, but meanwhile we learned to step over it. If we forgot, it reminded us. Since the elevator kept doing its job and other things needed Dad's fixing, we eventually accepted the elevator's idiosyncrasy and ceased to think it needed fixing, accepting it the way we accepted the grumpy cats who periodically scratched us.

A silo is a round, hollow cylinder, usually made of curved cement blocks, though sometimes made of steel. Ours was a small one, about thirty-five feet high. Every year we filled it with green corn, the entire plant cut off a couple inches above the ground and chopped into bits. We hauled these wagonloads of green corn to the silo and emptied them into the silage blower, essentially a big fan run off a long belt on the International "H." A metal pipe about eight inches in diameter ran from the blower to the top of the silo, and the blower literally blew the corn up the pipe and into the silo.

When I was younger I loved it when the blower plugged. It meant that the pipe had to be disconnected, the silage dug out, and the remainder blown out without the pipe in place. It shot out of the blower like a geyser, spraying silage high into the air, a wonderful thing to see.

We didn't start feeding silage for several months after chopping corn, supplying the cattle's roughage with hay instead. During those months the chopped corn underwent a transformation. The top three feet, exposed to air, rotted and turned into a stinking black mush. In doing so, however, it sealed oxygen away from the remainder, which consequently underwent an anaerobic fermentation instead of an aerobic rotting. The fermentation preserved all the nutrients but changed the nature of the feed.

If you enter a silo while the silage is fermenting, the gases can kill you. Every year several farmers in the Midwest die in just this way, going into a silo to fetch, say, a dropped tool, thinking they won't be there long enough to die. They quickly succumb to the powerful gases, falling unconscious. Once the fermentation is complete, however—the green corn turned brown, and the excess juice drained to the bottom of the silo—the smell of silage is rich and deep, with a hint of intoxication. Sweet and sour both, it is wine vinegar, quickened yeast, pickled vegetables, mown lawns.

Every year we filled the silo and every year we emptied it, forkful by forkful. Most farmers had silo unloaders, machines that hung from the roof of the silo by cables and ran around the silo, augering up the silage and blowing it out the doors. Dad couldn't afford a silo unloader, but he had sons, so every year, in late fall, we climbed up the galvanized chute, opened the topmost small door and, with overshoes on, stepped into the silo.

We removed the sheet of plastic covering the silage, which helped seal out oxygen, and with silage forks—broad pitchforks with tines spaced about an inch apart—threw out the top three feet of rotten, black, stinking corn. We threw this into a manure spreader and hauled it out to the fields. Once we hit the good, rich silage we placed the electric elevator under the chute and began the months of unloading the silo.

When we first began feeding silage and again when we ended, we had enough natural light from the small square of glass in the galvanized roof to see what we were doing, but most of the work in the silo was dark, winter work, done under a trouble light in mornings before sunrise.

Our breath preceded us up the chute. The second one up would wait for the first to disappear through the small door at the top, to keep from having silage kicked down on his head. Once through the door we entered a strange world, cut off, enclosed, contained. The first one up would grope in the dark until he found the trouble light, then switch it on. His shadow, cranky, grotesque, would shoot out from his feet, crooked-limbed, over the silage and up the curved walls. Two silage forks leaned against the cement. When the second brother had crawled through the door, the work began.

We removed the silage in eight-inch layers, starting at the door and working our way across the silo, one of us working the right side, the other the left, keeping the surface level, and alternating throwing the silage through the door. Kevin is left-handed, I right, Joel left, Colin right, so it was easy to form teams that worked well on opposite sides of the door. Early in the season the silage was light, getting more packed as we went down, but as winter deepened it began to freeze along the cement wall, at first a narrow ring that we removed with forks, but by January this ring was three feet thick and hard as granite.

Then one of us worked full-time chipping it away with a pickax, or an ax head Dad had welded in line to the end of a heavy metal pipe. It was like mining for silage—above ground rather than below, but confined within a narrow, dark tunnel, devoted to removing chips of material. I wondered aloud once why we didn't just leave the frozen silage along the wall, throw out the middle stuff, and wait for spring to thaw the rest. Dad pointed out that if we did that we'd find ourselves in the spring working underneath cliffs of unstable silage that could suddenly loosen and bury us.

Eventually Dad bought a secondhand silage chipper, a mole-like machine that looked like a small snowblower without the chute, and which we pulled backward across the frozen silage, the chipper's toothed auger biting into the frozen silage, bucking and kicking and fighting the person pulling it. It was almost as much work as a pickax, but faster.

We worked our way down. The cement cylinder grew around us, the galvanized roof where we'd started now high and distant. As spring came the silage thawed. Not having to chip seemed a luxury. We worked around the chipper until we reached the bottom door, then we shoved it out and stuck it in a corner of the feed shed, where it sat until next year.

By then light had returned. The silo was no longer cluttered with extension cords for the chipper and trouble light. We worked down into the pit, under the faraway light from the roof, the silage growing more pungent, sharp as good German sauerkraut, soggy from the collected juices, until we finally had to wear overshoes, as we had when we'd started. To get out of the pit we

pulled ourselves up and scrambled over the door ledge
on our stomachs, trying not to touch the shorted-out
elevator as we clambered over it.

Finally we felt the ground with our forks, underneath several inches of brown, vinegary water. We
threw the forks out the door and followed them into
the open spring and the smell of new alfalfa hay growing in the fields. Over the summer the silo dried out.
Redheaded woodpeckers clattered their beaks against
the metal roof, making a huge racket. I had the sense
they banged on the silo not because they hoped for insects but because they loved the sound, impressing
themselves with the noise they could make. We took
our cue from the birds—a firecracker dropped into the
silo, and held before it was dropped so that it exploded
halfway down, made a noise like a ton of dynamite. It
was great fun around the Fourth of July, with corn thick
and greening in the fields.

Stuck

The drift was a good forty yards long, heaving itself up out of the dredge ditch, which itself was full of snow, and across the road like an immense, slumbering snake. We couldn't see the ditches or the road, just a white blankness stretched out before the car the moment Kevin turned south, about a mile from our place.

School hadn't been canceled. Parents in those days weren't the suing types, and were more likely to get upset if a superintendent canceled school when it wasn't necessary than if he didn't when it was. If school wasn't canceled Mom and Dad figured we ought to go, so we were all packed into the '62 Chevy Impala—white, with a cracked, red vinyl interior, a six-banger for a power plant, and a three-speed in the column—a car Kevin detested for its lack of speed.

He stopped as soon as he turned the corner, and we

all stared at the drift. We were pretty used to snowdrifts. It took a good one to make us stare.

"I think we should go the other way," I said.

There were two problems with these words, neither having to do with the value of the suggestion itself. The first was that "the other way" was longer. It involved going a quarter mile north, then turning east and going past the Menk place to get to the highway rather than going south here and taking Ma Turney's road. Double a quarter mile and you have a half mile, a painful detour for Kevin at that time. Mom's favorite saying was "Patience is a virtue," a thing she usually said when something was particularly frustrating one of us and which generally made us erupt. Luckily, though, she never said patience was the *only* virtue, or Kevin wouldn't have had any.

The second major problem with my suggestion was that I was Kevin's younger brother and therefore didn't know anything. Had he arrived at my conclusion on his own, the drift would have remained large and unassailable, but my words contained a magic power that shrunk that drift down to a mere finger of snow lying on the ground.

"I'm not going around," Kevin growled at me. "I can get through that."

Doom managed to squeeze into the car and find a place, even though we were already packed shoulder to shoulder, the ones at the windows sitting sideways to breathe. No one said anything. Even Renee kept her mouth shut. Usually she argued with Kevin about everything, but this time, when argument might have been useful, she didn't say a word.

"All I need's a run for it," Kevin said.

A gust of wind hit the car. Snow flung itself out of Tubby Irlbeck's field and for a moment blinded us. The car rocked on its shocks, bad from being driven too fast over washboard roads.

A run for it. I looked at the snowdrift again, when the wind had blown past, and wondered if Kevin and I were talking about the same drift. A train would need a run for it. And anyway, I remembered that Dad had once told me that he went through snowdrifts slowly rather than fast, because too much speed would just make the car go out of control. As Kevin backed down the road, the Impala's transmission whining above the wind through the weather stripping, I tried to remember whether Kevin had been in the car during that conversation. If he had, I could appeal to his memory. If not, Dad's advice was hearsay.

I got no help from my siblings. Renee seemed to think that Kevin's plan was feasible—but Renee, though great at arguing, had no mind for snowdrifts. I found this out a couple of years later when she and I were both in town for a school event. The drifts were bad coming home, and after the first one Renee asked me to drive—which I did—though I didn't yet have my license. When I got home I told Mom I'd done so, joking about it, knowing she wouldn't believe me but protecting myself in case she found out later.

Joel and Colin were just young enough to think, as Kevin backed down the road, that we were engaged in something like a carnival ride, with a trusty carny—Kevin—at the controls. And Ann and Cyndee were oblivious to what was going on, since they were pretty much buried in the back seat.

Kevin backed the car up until he was a couple hundred yards from the drift. Snow swept in a curtain over Tubby Irlbeck's field, across the road above the drift, and into the dredge ditch. Kevin shoved in the clutch and moved the transmission to first. I made up my mind. "Dad says . . . ," I began.

Perhaps if I'd kept my mouth shut Kevin would have noticed the magnitude of the situation, or realized we were already halfway to the other road, or found some good excuse to change his mind and make it seem like he'd known all along what he was doing. But when I said, "Dad says," I forced him to take action. Having a younger sibling know anything is bad enough, but having one know what a parent would say—in other words, making a claim to actual wisdom—is intolerable.

So Kevin popped the clutch. The car lurched forward, almost died, lurched, almost died again. Inside it, seven staring heads went back and forth in unison, like seven perfectly timed pendulums with glasses on. Nothing made Kevin angrier than an engine without power. "Come on!" he yelled, and grimly floored the pedal. The car lurched once more, and then the threatened engine reluctantly took off.

If you can call it "taking off." Perhaps the most that can be said is that our heads stabilized. I'm sure Kevin had imagined the car achieving great speed by the time it hit the drift and flying through it in a victorious whiteout, but the Impala always managed to achieve less than anyone imagined for it. Loaded down as it was, it was superlative in its underachievement. Kevin managed to hit third gear, maybe forty-five miles an hour—though that's still too fast to be slamming into a packed drift.

The car hit. Seven pendulums with glasses swung shockingly forward. The car never had a chance. Before we knew what was happening, the Impala was skewed thirty degrees toward the dredge ditch, buried to its headlights twenty yards into the drift. Six of us were silent and in awe, staring through our glasses as the snow settled around us. Kevin wasn't silent at all.

I might have opened my mouth at that time and finished telling him what Dad said. I refrained.

Grunting and swearing by turns, Kevin pushed against the snow blocking his door, managed to open it, and squeezed out. Snatching the key from the ignition, he went to the trunk and yanked out the scoop shovel we carried there. He started flinging snow up from around the car as furiously as a terrier after a badger. One by one the rest of us climbed out and stood silently by, watching.

After fifteen minutes of exhausting labor, during which time Kevin had moved more snow than most people move in an entire winter, the car was still buried, the drift still huge. The only real change the shoveling effected was that he was too out of breath to continue swearing.

It was pretty clear to all of us that he wasn't going to get the car out of the drift until about midafternoon. He stood next to the car puffing, beads of sweat on his forehead in spite of the bitter wind. The rest of us watched him the way you might watch a box you suspect to be a bomb, afraid to move in case vibrations set off the detonator.

Had Mom been there, it would have been a great opportunity for her to exercise her favorite saying. "Patience is a virtue," she might have chirped to Kevin. In her absence, however, Fate sent Someone Else.

A car drove over the hill to the north—the Billmeier boys setting off to school a little later than we. They put on their turn signal at Menk's road but then noticed us and came straight ahead instead. The car inched up to the drift and stopped.

Tim Billmeier unfolded himself from the driver's seat. A year older than Kevin, he was as unlike my brother as anyone could be. Tall, thin, immensely polite, quiet to the point of shyness, Tim Billmeier never forced his opinion on anyone. He stood near the hood of his car, his hands in his pockets, and surveyed the scene: six grade-schoolers huddled near a buried car, their vision obscured by the snow sticking to their glasses; the car itself with taillights just visible above the snow; the fishtailing progress of its tracks into the drift; and my older brother puffing like a steam engine, red in the face, snow scattered around him like a bombing, and displaying all the signs, to anyone who knew him, of blowing up himself.

Tim Billmeier didn't know him. He looked at this scene for several seconds, took it all in, hunched his shoulders to drive his hands more deeply into his pockets.

"Are you *stuck*?" he asked.

A Constellation
of Cockleburs

I can still bring to mind the names and shapes and characteristics of the weeds that we had to pull by hand from the soybean fields when I was younger. My father was the most meticulous man in Redwood County at keeping his fields clean, capable of seeing from ten rows away a cocklebur, only a slightly lighter shade of green than the soybeans, hidden in a row being walked by one of his children. We were, of course, complaining about the humidity, heat, and mosquitoes, and the lumpy soil under our feet, and the length of the round and the number of weeds, and it didn't help to have it pointed out that we'd just missed another cocklebur.

"Where?!" I'd demand, as if Dad were creating, not just seeing, the weeds.

"Right behind you."

I'd turn and see nothing, just a row of soybeans. He'd direct my eyes, walk me with his voice, until I stood right over the weed and couldn't help but notice it, the cocklebur leaves broader than soybean leaves, more wavy-edged, with a shiny, black-spotted stem. Eventually, through such ongoing vigilance, Dad trained my eyes to see the contrast between cocklebur and soybean leaves so well that driving by on the road I could spot cocklebur in a field.

So I learned the names and shapes of other weeds—smartweed and pigweed and milkweed, wild hemp and Canada thistle, wild morning glory, crabgrass, quackgrass, foxtail—and whether they liked shade or sun, lay low or stood high, and how they propagated, some by explosive seeds, some by wind, some by dog- or combine-carried burs. And propagate they did. One cocklebur, its seeds allowed to ripen and then run through a combine, was capable of turning next year's field into depressing hours of stoop labor, the fecundity of weeds an abject lesson in why, if you're going to do a job at all, you ought to do it well.

But perhaps this last is myth rather than fact, our imaginations' projection of fecundity allowed to teach the lesson, since my father never allowed us to miss a cocklebur, or if he did and saw it standing tall and bur-laden in front of the combine, he would always stop the machine, pull the plant up and, carrying it carefully so as not to drop a single bur, bring it back to the tractor to burn later. Cocklebur had mythical stature, and the possible rupture of the myth into our lives, the fear of its realization, led to all sorts of rituals that farmers adhered to with the faith of fanatic priests.

My own father, his faith reserved for the Catholic

church, and the ritual there enough for any single lifetime, kept his cocklebur ritual small. Yet he kept it, paying homage to the power of the weed, teaching us that
cocklebur must never be cut off as volunteer corn could
be cut off. Cocklebur we had to pull out whole. The
hair roots snapped quietly, the soil sighed as the plant
came up.

But it wasn't enough to merely pull the plant out.
Cocklebur could resurrect itself from death. It was the
phoenix of weeds. If you left the ball of soil on the
roots—so we were taught, so the story went—and set
the plant down, the roots would live long enough to
reroot the plant, and within a few days the stem you'd
left lying on the ground would curve upright, and the
cocklebur would live again its pale-green threat in your
field, trembling again and always at the edge of living
eruption.

The ritual to contain such power was this: pull the
plant up whole, then hold it by the stem and beat it
with a cornhook so that the dirt chunked off and rained
down on the soybeans, and the white, spiraled roots, no
longer fleshed in soil, like a skeleton emerging from a
wasted body, lay quivering with each hit of the hook.
Then lay the plant upside down on the row of soybeans,
the denuded roots resting high in the air on top of the
vines and leaves. This last step had to be done carefully,
almost tenderly. If done carelessly, the plant might fall
off, the roots contact the ground again, and the plant
would spring to life renewed.

With tenderness, certainly with respect, perhaps
with a little awe, we laid the plant down on the soybean

row. Perhaps I'm going too far—or am I?—in seeing the row as an altar and the plant a sacrifice, and all of it a ritual, though never named, to control the fecund force that could devastate us—a ritual not that much different from the scattering of blue corn pollen upon the deer killed by the Navajo, not that much different from the prayer offered to the animal's spirit. For those rituals, too, must be—to those who practice them—ordinary and common and purely necessary as well as holy, part of the way one controls or appeases forces, the small gods such as Cocklebur that shape our lives when we truly belong to a place.

Dad practiced only small cocklebur rituals, but think of the farmers less meticulous or less trained in their eyesight, who let cocklebur grow in their fields until it stood, brown and brittle, above the soybeans, with hundreds of burs on a plant. These farmers had to gather the plants, now too obvious and tangled and devilish for even the least imaginative to ignore, and carry them to a barren, open place, piling them one upon another, brittle stalk upon brittle stalk, thousands of burs—hard, curled germs of a difficult future—until the pile was three or four feet high.

Then, in a strange blend of the purely practical and the ritualistic, the technological and mystical, they poured gasoline over the pile, struck a match, and tossed it. In an instant the pyre warped the air, and for a while the farmer watched, having paid the hard, workaday homage to the weed. How can we not see, even if the farmer didn't, sacrificial altars of appeasement going back thousands of years? Looking the other way, through the flame and wavy air, can we distinguish the farmer in his bright, seed-corn cap or straw hat and denim coat from his feather-and-fur-clad neolithic ancestor, or from Abel, or from Cain?

Technology has diminished Cocklebur, working away at the little gods. Herbicides have weakened the summer ritual of walking beans, of paying stoop homage to the weeds. But gods, even small ones, have ways of slipping through our technological hands, shifting like Proteus wakened near the sea. Canada thistle, which in my youth had the same mythical tenacity as cocklebur and was harder to pull, requiring leather gloves, has moved westward across the plains. Ranchers in Wyoming speak of it with awe and admiration as it takes over their pastures. I, a town dweller now and therefore not expected to know of such things, keep my silence when I hear them talk, though they're talking about one of my blood-and-bones gods. I could impart to them the rituals that might keep it under control, though never destroy it.

From a hundred yards away, walking a path through virgin land around Devil's Tower, I've spotted Canada thistle, the purple blossoms on the tall stem. I've gone through the grasses and stood over it, thinking. My deliberation was partly moral, the deliberation of a knower-of-truth in a land of ignorance. Do you act on the truth you carry or on the ignorance of the place you're at?

Canada thistle is a member of the aster family. As I stood there, a butterfly alighted on the blossom. The signs ask you not to disturb the ecology around Devil's Tower. But this wasn't part of the original ecology. I remembered a neighbor who didn't pay enough attention to Canada thistle. One year he had to disc up three acres of soybeans in a desperate attempt to get rid of the thistles in them—an immense, nasty, tangled patch, an eruption of thorns that made my heart sink just seeing it. But if I pulled this thistle before me, I would have to pull that one too, and that one, and that one—as I looked around I saw more of them. I might never make it back to the car.

I wondered if the rangers knew what they were up against. I wondered if I should tell them. Imagining that I felt the foolishness that the prophets must have sometimes felt, I understood something of their courage. In a land of ignorance, knowledge can seem crazy. I could see myself marching in to tell the rangers the mythology of thistle. They would humor me, and agree that they should all drop everything and go with leather gloves on to pull thistles. They would look at each other when I left and shrug and say: "We get all kinds."

I left the thistle blooming. The butterfly didn't know it was a weed. And I've learned that small gods can be controlled only within a small enough area. The rituals take too much time, attention, and vigilance. They have to be learned as we learn the land, by slow walking and sweat, in the bend of our backs and the ongoing training of our eyes.

A few years ago, at the urging of my oldest son, I bought a medium-sized reflecting telescope with high-quality optics. We spent two months waiting for it, and when it finally arrived we rushed outside, set it up—

and found only the moon. I thought I knew the night skies well, but I'd never *had* to know them. Though I'd spent a good deal of time under the night skies when I was on the farm, walking up the driveway or field road alone in complete darkness unbroken by lights, I'd merely absorbed what it pleased me to absorb. Dad didn't plant crops or sell cattle by the stars, and I had neither myth nor practical reason to learn them, and no one to train my eyes. I'd thought that the telescope, merely by being a telescope, would increase and deepen my seeing, but I learned that first night that it required a new knowledge: I had to know what to look for, and where.

I discovered sky charts and began to pass time in the evenings studying them. I quickly found that the patterns of the constellations, which the charts make appear definite and unambiguous, are in fact no easier to see than a cocklebur among soybeans. The lines that form the constellations are arbitrary. Any number of other lines might serve as well, and these possible other lines crisscross and confuse you the moment you step outside to match what you think you know with what is.

Nevertheless, with the help of the star and planet charts, we found Saturn, Jupiter, Mars, and the Andromeda galaxy, nearly filling the lens. They were all abrupt and startling, and right where they should be. Then a new stage of ignorance entered. Whenever we tried to find fainter galaxies or star clusters, we were disappointed, no matter how hard we searched. I questioned the quality of the telescope. Finally I called an amateur astronomer I knew and asked for help. One cold winter night we went to his home. He examined

his charts in the kitchen, eyeing distances and relationships, then stepped into the night where the telescope
sat in the snow. He intended to find a pair of galaxies
in Ursa Major, galaxies I'd tried to find myself. He
peered through the finder, then into the main lens,
muttered, moved the scope around, and finally exclaimed: "Got 'em."

I peered into the lens. I saw stars and empty sky.
"What?" I asked. "I don't see anything."

"Right in the middle of the lens. Those two faint
patches. They look like smudges of light."

Then I saw them. I'd probably seen them before,
but hadn't. Their light had entered my eyes, but I
hadn't seen them; recognition and perception come si-
multaneously. Now, however, I became aware of faint
light. It gradually took on shape until I could make out
the galaxies, one facing me and the other edge-on. As
I continued to look they revealed more of their structure, until I wondered how I could have failed to see
them before.

In order to see, I'd needed a real teacher, a real set
of eyes that would make me look and look again, past
my ignorance and frustration to the world that entered
my eyes. Once recognized, the pattern once known, I
could cast it before me, just as, trained by my father, I
learned to expect cocklebur. The faintest smudge now
reveals itself as a galaxy or nebula. I first had to learn
what to look for, then where, and finally how.

My knowledge of the night skies, however, has become
even more layered. I bought the telescope to see invisible and specific points, but in a totally unexpected turn-

about, the greatest change in my awareness concerns the way I see and know the whole sky, the way it sweeps around the pole, and the way I feel and respond to its rhythms.

Since childhood, Orion has been my favorite constellation. Randall Jarrell calls it "the cold Hunter, Orion, wheeling upside down, all space and stars, in cater-cornered heaven." Jarrell captures the way that Orion so dominates the sky that the heavens seem to tip to adjust to it. The great hunter appears with his dogs at the beginning of winter and makes his way, night by night, star-stride by star-stride, across the cold skies.

This past spring, on a warm April evening, I stepped out my back door and saw the Hunter hanging low over Crow Peak in the Black Hills west of my house, dwarfing the mountain—but about to set—just as evening began. I was suddenly filled with a strange, quiet grief and expectation. I knew I was going to miss Orion's familiar, angled presence above me. At the same time I knew he would be replaced by the Summer Triangle of Altair, Vega, and Deneb. But beyond, and deeper than all thought, I had the odd but real feeling that Orion was physically pushing winter before him as he moved, forcing the season right now over the edge of the world, somewhere behind Crow Peak, leaving the skies available to spring. This rich, full sense of a connection between earth and sky, between the near and far, sight and feeling—this sense of being within and participating in the change of the heavens— must surely be what all people who have identified patterns in the stars and explained them in stories must have felt.

It is possible to buy a motor mount for a telescope

that compensates for the earth's rotation and keeps the scope centered on an object in the lens. Without such a mount, however, you get to feel the earth move under you. What most surprises people when they first look through a telescope is that an object won't stay in the lens for more than a half minute. "It's moving," I've had friends exclaim, and when I told them they were noticing the earth's rotation, magnified thirty or a hundred times, they stepped away from the scope and looked around as if unsure where they were.

They had suddenly become aware of the planet on which they stood, how it spins at terrific, huge, and silent speed. The sun rises and sets, the moon and stars appear and fade into light, but we don't notice. Once you start to search for specific points in the sky, however, the feeling of movement is driven into you. Eventually my awareness of this vast rhythm led me to want to know the stories of the sky and how people identified with them. All cultures have known the skies, have named and storied them, and I might have chosen from among many systems of lines and configurations, but because the names I had come to know from the star charts were from the ancient Greek, I began to reread Greek mythology with my son to understand not just what, but who, we were looking at. They are all up there—Perseus, Andromeda chained to her rock, the sea monster who comes to devour her, and Cassiopeia her mother and Cepheus her father. Isaac Newton himself noted that the voyage of Jason and the Argonauts is retold in the signs of the zodiac, and wondered whether the story went back to ancient Egypt. And Orion is a hunter destroyed by Apollo for getting too close to

Artemis, pursued by the Scorpion at the opposite end of the heavens.

As an adult now, I find myself repeating with the stars the pattern of knowledge acquisition I experienced as a child with the glaciers—the knowledge of intellect and science turning gradually into a knowledge of story and a felt sense of place and time, mystery and belonging. Just as, through the sweat and toil of picking up rocks, I eventually felt the glacier's deep, abiding presence on the land, and myself as part of it, so, through sitting on snowy ground or warm summer grass in darkness, peering through a lens, the ancient Greek sky has become my sky—not merely *the* sky but *my* sky, personal, familiar, patterned. When I step under it and look up, I'm oriented. I fit, like something clicking into place. I belong to the pattern, and because I've come to know it, it belongs to me. When I see the night sky, it is no longer random points of light but a living world, passionate and intelligent. Because of this, just as the glacier, though long past, still broods upon the northern prairie, so the world of the ancient Greeks exists in the present, alive and whole, breathing in the wind and darkness of the North American plains. Stories—the powerful ones, the mythical ones—have this kind of potency to transform us and our worlds, to shift time and remake space, and lodge us where we are.

My father never thought to eradicate Canada thistle and cocklebur by our annual return to the soybean fields. He *knew* that every year he would return. As a child I thought that such ritual, recurring work trapped me, was inflexible and boring. But one has to learn to appreciate any form of beauty, to know its nuances. Walking soybeans brought us to touch the land, to live in the place we lived upon. It was a family affair, all of us, brothers and sisters, drawn together by mutual purpose. In fact, the entire community was involved, with farmers hiring teenagers and children from town to help with a job too large for any individual. Just as the combines appeared in our driveway in the recognition of communal necessity, so in a smaller way, before the invention of powerful herbicides, entire farming communities recognized the potency of the small weed-gods and shifted their patterns and relationships in response to them. The definition of "farmer" and "town dweller" broke down, and the entire community mixed and shared the work. Out of necessity and ritual work, a different kind of freedom emerged, a different kind of beauty and truth and even goodness.

Many summers we had to walk soybeans three times, the weeds a steady, patient, and enduring force. With the end of that third, despairing walk, the fields lay flat and even, nothing malignant or nasty sticking above it. God! What a relief to have it over, done with, finished. But my father knew, and I know now, that with the circling of the seasons we'd be out again, responding—pulling up weeds and beating the roots and laying the weeds down, with the mosquitoes in our ears and the sun in the sky, with my older brother's transistor radio—strapped to his belt and turned to KDWB in Minneapolis—playing the Beatles and the Rolling Stones, tinny and clangy and ineffective six or seven rows away, its sound carried away by the wind.

You don't pull cockleburs and Canada thistle year
after year and watch them return each summer without coming to distrust fixings and finalities, remembering how clean the fields were the summer before.
You don't watch the weeds marching clear across the
plains in their small-god steadfastness without coming
to accept that some things are more enduring than
you are, some forces too patient and potent and alive
for eradication.

I live now at the edge of town, where it is dark enough
that a lot of stargazing can be done in our backyard,
even though many fainter objects in the sky are
blocked by the lights of the town. The summer we first
got the telescope I put it in the car one night and took
Derek and his six-year-old sister Lauren away from
town. We took the first gravel road we found and drove
until it dropped over a rise, and all the lights of town
disappeared.

I stepped from the car and stood in the middle of
the road, the huge heavens wheeling over me, the
Milky Way sharp and white. Derek came out and
looked up and began to laugh. He twirled and turned,
laughing, amazed at the immensity and clarity. Then
Lauren came out of the car. She looked up, and without
a word came to me and clung to my leg.

"What do you think?" I asked.

"I'm scared," she said in a small voice.

She held tighter under the dizzying reaches that
made her so small. She needed to hold on so that she
wouldn't be swept up and away. She was feeling the

sky's ancient power, which you feel sometimes even as an adult. Standing on the prairie with the wind blowing over you, you can feel that you could be picked up and blown into the heavens. The prairie's gravity doesn't seem strong enough to stop it. Then you remember, if you know them, stories of just such things happening to people familiar to you—and you look up and see them there, striding over you. You can be filled with fear and wonder: do you belong down here, or up there, among the stars?

My children don't have weeds to pull, but perhaps they will have memories of standing with their father, unable to see a constellation as it is pointed out to them again and again, until it finally dawns in their awareness and sight. They will know, I hope, that they can't still the sky, and that the stories the skies tell are myths they can't afford to lose. The stories could be from any culture, and the pictures that illustrate them above us could be formed in different ways, but from any culture the meaning would be the same—that the skies above us are the skies of history, the skies of people who lived upon and cared for the earth long before us and knew its forces and changes as part of their lives.

The darkest night I've ever been in was one during my adolescence. Some friends and I were catfishing the Minnesota River until well past midnight on a cloudy, moonless night. When we began the half-mile hike through the woods to our cars it was literally pitch-black, and none of us had brought a flashlight. We entered the woods and stopped, unable to see the trees, unable to see each other, unable to move. We stood still and discussed our dilemma, our voices quiet and disembodied in the overwhelming darkness. Then I had the idea to use a fishing pole like a cane to avoid trees, and to work our way out of the woods.

In spite of my poor sense of direction, since it was my idea I was chosen to lead. Swinging the fishing pole in a half circle before me, I set off, the others following like a train, each with his fingers hooked in the belt loop of the person in front of him. The click of pole against bark guided me. I pulled us up the hill by feel and sound, never seeing a thing, and we found our cars, and then told and retold the story. Only later did we learn that the farmer who owned that land had pastured a bull with a famous temper in the meadow on top of the bluff.

We had apparently escaped through pure luck, but the possibility became part of our story, the danger we had avoided part of the experience and memory, the sudden eruption of the bull out of the darkness as I stumbled upon it with my fishing pole part of what we told. Taurus the Bull is in the sky, solidifying every winter, carrying the jewel of the Hyades in his head. If I could story the sky to my personal taste and life, I would leave him there, and Orion the Hunter as well, but I would also find, perhaps, Cocklebur and Canada Thistle, the Farmer with the Straw Hat and His Unseeing Son, Leather Glove and Cornhook, Alighting Butterfly. And Milkweed would explode and Smartweed would run like a thread through the night, and the Milky Way would be their bright, potent seeds. The Farmer and his

Son would be forever watching and vigilant, circling back every year to their wide star fields after a rest below the horizon. But even in the winter the Pleiades would be a reminder that nothing ever ends or is finished, a single Bright Bur that they missed.

Black Snow

Ever since John Deere invented the steel moldboard plow, which allowed the tough prairie sod to be broken, it has remained, until recent years, the primary way to till soil. Dad used one, but because it turned the soil over, leaving it black and uncovered, blizzard winds scoured it, mixing it with snow to form "snirt"—black snow that drifted into road ditches and in the spring melted to mud.

Fields plowed in the fall yielded better crops than those plowed in the spring. The soil warmed sooner, winter freezing made it softer and more tillable, and it could be planted earlier, with longer-maturing, higher-yielding corn hybrids. Fall plowing was a hectic time. We often plowed late into the night, keeping the tractors going, the weak lights illuminating only the wheel running down the furrow, and the plow behind sliding through the soil, lifting it in a graceful black wave, turning it over.

One fall I stood with Dad just after we'd finished fall plowing, looking over the blackened land. I felt great satisfaction having the job done, and I said so.

"Yes," Dad replied, "but it's no good."

I didn't understand. I thought having the work done was an automatic good. He must have seen my confusion.

"All that soil turned to the wind all winter. It erodes. We really shouldn't plow in the fall. But I don't know what to do about it."

He silenced me. We stood together for a moment, looking at the black land transformed by our labors and then, for me, transformed again by his comment. It hadn't occurred to me that our farm—flat, thick-soiled, muscular with humus—was susceptible to erosion. With one small comment he changed the way I looked at the farm, made me see it as something vulnerable, tender, easily bruised, affected by so minor a thing as whether we plowed in the fall or the spring. I'd never thought there was a decision to be made in that, never thought there was a choice.

With the comment he made, Dad changed not only the way I looked at the land but the way I looked at him. I'd thought he was a farmer, whose mind was on farming, on the tasks he had to do and when he had to do them. I discovered suddenly that he was a thinker— a reflecter, a wonderer, a worrier—who thought not only of the present but of the future, even the future beyond his life, and of how the things he did affected that future world. It surprised me to realize that he carried

such thoughts—an undercurrent of debate within himself about his relationship to what he did and owned—
all the time he was feeding cattle or pulling weeds or
driving a tractor up and down the fields.

Dad was a quietly fervent Catholic. Though the
Catholic church was at that time weighted toward the
preaching of sin and guilt, and toward itself as the sole
salvation from sin, both my parents slipped through this
potential barrier to a deeper belief. Dad attended to all
the rituals—the holy days, the obligatory Sundays, the
rules and observances, the fasts and abstinences, the
schedules for confession—but he did it not out of fear
alone, but because he believed in the rituals' positive,
transforming presence in his life.

Because he both believed and observed, the rituals
were transformative. A nun once commented to Joel
and Colin's class that there was this man who, when he
came back from communion on Sundays, looked like a
saint, and the class should aspire to that kind of awareness of the Presence Within. Wanting her students to
observe her model, she repeated the description several
weeks in a row, until Joel and Colin realized she was
talking about Dad. We had a wonderful time with that,
laughing at this nun who would think our dad was a
saint, when the truth was, he was our dad. Her opinion
would change, we thought, if she knew he was the father of Joel and Colin who, far from being the sons of a
saint, were students.

That nun was on to something, though; when Dad
returned from communion, he had an expression as
peaceful as a human can have. Yet when he made that
comment about fall plowing, the land eroding, and his

inability to do much about it, he moved me beyond the parameters of sin and the auspices of the Church, though at the time I didn't understand this, and it surely wasn't his intention.

My discomfort at his comment was multilayered—not simply that I lost the satisfaction of a huge job done, or that I was participating in ecological degradation, or even that my father was revealed to me as someone far more complex and subtle than I knew. Though all these were part of my uneasiness, overriding them all, in ways I couldn't pin down, was the sense that Dad, this believer and keeper-of-the-rituals, was concerned with problems the belief and rituals didn't address. And they weren't just problems of practicality; they were problems of right and wrong.

I had no trouble understanding the choice laid out in his comment. He farmed two hundred acres. In order to raise his family on so little land, he had to make the land produce as much as he could. Fall plowing allowed higher corn yields than spring plowing and was therefore necessary. Yet he *ought* to have been spring plowing. It was the *right* thing to do. He looked across the black, fall fields and saw not increased wealth and a good job done, as I did, but a coming, long-term poverty, the loss of the farm itself to the wind—lost to him, lost to his family, lost to the future—the most enduring and stable thing I knew turned to air and dust, and turned that way through cause, by something he could prevent.

"But I don't know what to do about it," he said, and turned his face from where it had been looking over the fields, the land stretching blackly away to the horizon. He turned his face away to another task that needed doing, and I followed him, two steps behind, my world changed.

Joseph Campbell writes that it is impossible for a human being to live and not feel guilty. Our lives depend on the deaths, plant or animal, of other beings. The old myths, and the rituals associated with them, allow us to acknowledge that guilt, to expiate it, and to affirm that life is good. Growing up on a farm is an experiential lesson in the truth of Campbell's observation. Everything you touch and care for and even learn to love is touched and cared for and even loved so that it will die at the time you have appointed—the leghorn roosters with their brief, proud weeks of life, passionately loved and fed and then dispassionately slaughtered and eaten; the cattle upon whom everything revolves— named, identified, tamed—to be judged, finally, with a critical eye and put on the night trucks; even the crops planted season after season so that, season after season, they will mature and die.

Nothing on a farm is intended to last more than a year. Almost all of the work is done within a yearly cycle. Only the cycles themselves, and the land that supports them, are meant to endure. When I was twelve and thirteen years old, this caused a sort of despair in me.

We used small equipment; the Five-Sixty pulled "four fourteens," the Super M "three sixteens"—a four-bottom plow, each bottom, or share, fourteen inches wide, or fifty-six inches total, and three sixteen-inch shares for forty-eight inches total. Nothing I've ever done has quite produced the same sinking feeling in me as when I was younger and went out to the large north field and laboriously, at about two-and-a-half miles an hour, pulled a plow through the ground for a quarter mile, then reached the other end of the field and made the turn and saw that puny, four-foot-wide black strip lying in the center of a half-mile field of cornstalks. Not only did the task of plowing the field once seem to stretch into eternity—the thought of its impermanence was like lead in my heart. I was going to plow that entire field, and in a year I'd have to do it all again, and then again, and again.

I learned, of course, that if I just kept going, the work got done; those four-foot strips became eight, and sixteen, and eventually the whole field was turned over. Such work can't help but give a child a feeling of power and self-control, of an ability to make a difference in the world. Yet it was always mingled with the realization that it never ended, that every year returned it, and that the difference I made was relative to time.

It's an astonishing thing, as a child, to be part of transforming an entire landscape, to see the green tips of the corn emerge, to overwhelm, and in the old Catholic phrase, to "renew" the face of the earth. Yet underneath the sense of power, dignity, and strength that such transforming work gave me, was a deeper heartthrob and pang: none of it lasts. It's all done so that it will die and be harvested, and winter will return, and then the work again.

Sorrow, guilt, compassion, despair; dignity, joy, appreciation, love. If Campbell is right, the old myths and rituals served to help humans integrate these conflicting sets of emotions and their attendant realizations: as individuals we die, and until we die we live on the deaths of other individuals; but it's wonderful to live nevertheless, it's wonderful to have the chance to die, it's wonderful to eat and feed others, it's all tragic and yet calls us to rejoice.

My father's comment that fall day, however, took all of this to a new, and as yet unexplored and dangerous level, one that the old myths and rituals, growing more slowly than our technical knowledge, have not become fully capable of handling. My father wasn't expressing just deep sorrow at having to sell cattle for slaughter in order to maintain his own life and ours. That sorrow is a known one—gentling, humbling, never dismissed but never incapacitating. He was expressing instead confusion over the possibility that in maintaining his own life and the lives of those he loved, he was taking not just other individual lives but the entire base upon which all those lives depended, and he was doing it consciously, knowingly—and yet helplessly.

The confusion went beyond any concept of sin I'd ever learned. Sin, being a known thing, wasn't talked about. One was supposed to recognize one's sins, not debate them. In the pews were booklets with long lists of sins in categories—a taxonomy of wrongdoing—provided not to help you decide before confession *whether* you'd committed certain sins, but to help you *remember* that you had.

I couldn't imagine my parents sinning. Once when I was in fourth grade, as my mother prepared to go to confession, I wondered aloud why she bothered. Sin was something done primarily against parents' desires and commands. "What kinds of sins can you commit?" I asked her.

"Oh, more than you," she replied.

Her sincerity was clear to me. Still, I didn't understand. She never fought, never held grudges, never lied or teased someone to the point of anger, never disobeyed (with no one to disobey)—and those were about the limits of my by now already memorized aids to an examination of conscience when I went to confession.

"But what?" I persisted.

She brushed her black hair back and checked her purse for something. "That's between me and God," she said.

Sin was private partly because it was assumed to be known. In fact, if you didn't know you were committing a sin, it wasn't a sin. Knowledge was part of the definition. But when Dad, a few years after I had this conversation with my mother, commented about the black fields, he opened a door into a new realm, oddly innocuous and yet worse than Sin, beside which a fight with my brother paled to insignificance and yet it meant nothing in ordinary life—a few grains of topsoil cast to the wind.

My father wouldn't work on Sundays, except to feed cattle and do necessary chores. Only a few times, when field work was urgent enough to demand Sunday work, did he find the priest after mass and ask for dispensation to work. Often on Sundays we watched neighbors' tractors crawl up and down the fields, or heard their dull hum, saw smoke from their stacks smudge the horizon, while we maintained silence and inactivity. There was in

this refusal to work a feeling of being, not morally superior, for our parents made it clear it was all right for our
neighbors to work on Sundays, but set apart.

As I grew older this feeling faded and was replaced
with cynicism. Children accept paradox, wise men understand it, teenagers reduce it to contradiction. I
couldn't see why God would hold us to different standards. Now I know it was my father upholding the standards. He decided, for himself, to abide by the rule
against work on Sundays; many Catholic farmers, then
and now, climbed aboard their tractors without much
thought on Sundays. In abiding by the rule, and agreeing to discuss it with the priest if he wished to work, he
forced himself to ask just what work *was* necessary.

Thus work was held in its place as an economic activity primarily, and subordinated to other values—religious, familial, communal. The standard helped Dad
reflect upon what he did to make a living. It aided in
making him a sort of farmer-philosopher, who had not
merely to act but also to think, and to think not only in
terms of profit and management, but of how his work
fit into larger concerns. Thus when he did work on
Sundays it became a sort of prayer, a renewed and
deepened understanding of his spiritual life, brought
on by the need to think deeply about whether this
work was financially necessary *enough* to override other
values.

When it came to fall versus spring plowing, however, he had no standard by which to abide. His religion
provided him with a flexible structure that helped him
reflect upon his day-to-day work and subordinate it to
larger meaning, but it provided him nothing in terms of

the more troublesome and insidious issues of environment and finances. Perhaps his comment to me that fall
day was the beginning of my own lifelong concern with
environmental issues, my awareness of the uneasy com-
promises I make, constantly and daily, between my
ideals and my practicality.

Modern farmers steer a strange course between the
Scylla of technology and the Charybdis of nature. Most
are strong conservationists who wish to preserve the
land, and also intense capitalists who need to squeeze as
much profit from the land, their investment, as they
can. Even as they try to distance themselves, through
technology, from nature, they are completely absorbed
in the natural world, which can at its whim destroy or
reward them. And increasingly they live, like all of us
do, with the knowledge that the technology they use
can change and even destroy their livelihood, and nature itself.

Since my family quit farming, technology has found
a way to deal with the problem of fall plowing. Few
farmers today use a moldboard plow. Instead they use
"no till" technology, loosening the soil with sweeps
dragged underground, but leaving the soil cover intact
to prevent wind erosion. Since this method doesn't bury
weed seeds, however, farmers rely on more, and more
powerful, herbicides than anything my father used.

The problem of wind erosion has been slowed, but
the environmental concerns continue, though more
subtle and less visible. The chemicals are supposedly
safe for the environment, but one has to wonder; in
farming country these days, entire counties are covered

with these chemicals, year after year. Is it possible to "test" the long-term effects of such widespread and continuous saturating of the land? Is it possible to test for all the possible, complex interactions?

I remember the satisfaction I took after the final beanwalking, after days in the hot sun, walking up and down the soybean rows, pulling individual weeds. We had to do this because soybeans, unlike corn, were un-resistant to any herbicide then invented. We looked across the fields when we were finished and saw not a single weed breaking the smooth, even surface. When I look across a soybean field today, however, I see it as my father saw the black, fall fields, and I wonder what the long-term effects are of such clean fields, produced through such potent technologies.

I want to believe that the chemicals are safe, as the chemical companies claim. One thing I do know, how-ever, is that no matter how safe they are, they are not as safe as walking soybeans and pulling weeds by hand. On the other hand, that was hard and difficult labor. On the other hand again, if there is one thing we've learned about technologies, it is that even with the most thor-ough tests their effects can be only partially predicted, if for no other reason than that we can only test for what we can imagine.

My father's dilemma, as he stared across the field that fall, is a modern dilemma, perhaps brought to its clearest point and contrast in farming, since the dependence on both nature and technology is so apparent there. Never-theless, it is anyone's dilemma. It is my dilemma—if I have my car's air conditioner refilled, as I watch the smoke from my wood stove go into the air, whenever I think of living further out in the country to enjoy the space but taking and developing more land to do it. None of it seems much, I know—a few grains of topsoil. Yet I'm constantly aware, as my father was, of what those few grains may mean.

The modern world has moved the truth of Campbell's observation into a new, wide realm. We're all too aware that we live, perhaps, upon widespread destruction, this awareness and doubt apparent even in the stridency of those who insist that we don't. We haven't learned to expiate the guilt and fear this creates, haven't developed the structures and rituals that allow us to reflect upon it and make decisions within a proper framework and subordination of values.

As a result, we continually cede the right to make these large decisions to the impersonal forces of science and economics—forces that are, unfortunately, informed by the concept of continual growth. This is again nowhere more evident than in farming. The chemical companies are now entering the field of recombinant DNA technology, splicing herbicide-resistant genes from other species into soybeans, so that a single spray from a powerful herbicide will suffice to produce a weed-free field and leave the soybeans intact. The chemical companies make up for the reduced sales of herbicide by patenting the seed and charging more for it, and the end result is that the farmer is more dependent on the corporation.

Even should such a technique be proven absolutely

free of environmental risk, its social and familial and even spiritual effects are grave. A farmer, instead of depending on his sons and daughters to help him clean his fields, now depends on a corporation. Instead of hiring local teenagers, he sends more and more of his money out of the community. Instead of being able to limit growth, he finds himself investing in more expensive technologies, which can only be supported by ever larger economies of scale.

As that investment increases, as more of the farmer's resources leave the community, he becomes more dependent for his thinking and decision making on the very technologies and economic ideas that have led him to his current condition. Of course it isn't farmers alone. It's all of us.

An important but almost never recognized fact about the way we use our money, resources, and time is that when we invest, we are ultimately investing in *ideas*. When a farmer hires community teenagers to help him bale hay or pull weeds or pick rock, he is investing in the idea of community, and in the idea that young people can accomplish meaningful work, in the idea that he and the teenagers have, at least for the time that the work lasts, a common purpose and way of seeing the world.

On the other hand, when he invests in herbicides and larger machinery, he is investing in the idea that technology can make his life easier, solve his problems, enrich him—but he is also investing in the idea that an increasing distance between him and his land and work is beneficial, and that his true community, the community he depends on for his survival, exists not in the people around him, his neighbors, but in the distant and impersonal world.

Even now, with the distance and safety of years between us, I'm not sure what my father might have done to resolve his dilemma. He was, as most farmers are, deeply invested in the financial system, a system that made it practically impossible for him to plow his fields in the spring. He was just as deeply, perhaps more deeply, invested in the Catholic church, the local community, and his family. But none of these institutions allowed investment in a powerful idea that could counteract the weight of the financial one, and none of them provided support—emotional, spiritual, or financial—for resistance to the demands of profit.

It seems to me that this is one of the major tasks for those institutions in the next fifty years. We need a definition of family that resists, at the basic level, the financial imperative to growth and consumption. We need communities that actively support land ethics and live within their environments quietly. Finally, we need our spiritual institutions to take on the huge challenge suggested by Campbell's observation, to move beyond the simple tragedy of mortality they have always dealt with, and grow to confront the immense tragedy of environmental and communal degradation, the tragedy that not only mere individual lives, but all life, life itself, may be harmed by our existence.

We need a mythical response to our environmental situation and to our current state of living on this planet. By "myth," I mean, of course, what Campbell means,

and what I've meant throughout these essays—powerful
stories that shape us, form us, ground us, identify us as
physical and spiritual beings who live in time but know
timelessness, and who are connected to all that we
see. It's a huge challenge, to discover and interpret such
myths—for I believe they are discovered, not made—
but in Joseph Campbell's spirit, it is a joyful challenge,
one of infinite potential, and one that can free us from
our helplessness.

Birds
Against the Glass

They rose from the freeway in front of me, white, gray, and blue, angling from the side of the road as if in slow motion, yet instinctively sure of their own speed, unable to comprehend anything faster. Yet they seemed to me, at seventy miles an hour, to be dragged down by air currents they hadn't expected, held in stasis in front of my windshield. I knew what was going to happen and ducked behind the windshield the moment before two of them exploded against the glass. They turned from birds to gray blurs rushing at me, to nothing but one small feather fluttering in a smear of blood. They'd come right at my face and would have killed or blinded me. I knew without slowing down that those two pigeons were dead. When you hit them that hard, you know.

I remembered a Sunday when I was a child. We were going to church, late as usual, the dust rolling behind us from the gravel road past Tubby Irlbeck's field, when I heard a *thunk* against the windshield and Dad pulled the Impala to the side of the road.

"What happened?"

"We hurt a bird," Mom explained.

"So what's he doing?"

"It's still alive. It flew into the ditch."

I didn't understand. Neither did anyone else in the car. We were unable to furnish the conclusion implied by her statement, and finally she said: "He's going to find it and kill it."

That silenced us. Dad left the car and, wearing a suit and good shoes, walked into the ditch. Tubby Irlbeck hadn't mowed his ditch yet and Dad sank knee-high into grass, milkweed, and thistle. He walked back and forth, his head down, in the long, dusty grass. It looked unhurried and peaceful, and it looked strange.

"He can't find it," Mom said.

"Maybe it's OK. Maybe it flew away."

"No."

Then Dad walked into Tubby Irlbeck's soybean field, not even his own field. Suddenly he ran a few steps, looking stranger all the time, running in his suit in a soybean field. He made a quick, stooping motion and shook something. Then he walked out of the field and got into the car.

"Did you find it?" Mom asked.

"Yes."

Mom reached over across the children sitting between them in the front seat and began to pick sand burs and bits of grass out of Dad's suit. He drove on, saying nothing, turned left on Ma Turney's road, heading for the highway. Mom went on plucking at the suit. When we reached the church we scrambled out. Normally we went in the side door, but today our parents led us to the front entrance.

"Why are we going this way?"

"Your father's got to wash his hands."

He went down to the basement while we milled in the vestibule. My parents didn't like walking into church late, but this time Mom seemed unconcerned. The opening hymn began, but we just stood there. Finally Dad walked back up the steps. Mom checked his suit one more time; then we walked, conspicuously late, up the side aisle to find a pew.

The path we take to gentleness is an enigmatic and convoluted one, and gentleness itself is hard to pin down. Dad walked into that field and with his bare hands killed a living thing, an act that might be considered cruel, and yet I regard it as one of the gentlest things I've ever known a man to do. On the way to church he stopped to finish a killing.

I'm sure he was tempted to let it go, to drive on, to make life easy for himself. Instead he stopped, and by so doing, without ever lecturing, he left me with no doubts that if you wound an animal you become responsible for its pain. It was a lesson of the highest sort, and the memory of him walking in that field, dressed in Sunday clothes, stands out in my moral imagination like a plain bulb in a white room. You are responsible for the things you do, it says—and even accidents are things you do.

As far as I can see, human beings are born neither

gentle nor cruel. They are born helpless. Gentleness and cruelty depend on power, on efficacy. We must learn gentleness, then—if we learn it—as we grow out of helplessness and discover that our actions can affect the pain or happiness of others.

Living on a farm as we lived on it, in constant and close contact with animals that depended on us, provided endless opportunities for gentleness or cruelty. I realize there are those who would say that merely raising an animal with the intent to kill and eat it is cruel at its core. Perhaps it is. If so, my life has been formed in inescapable cruelty. Yet I'm more interested here in those moments when cruelty and gentleness meet, when the line between them is so fine they almost become each other.

I used to love it when Dad killed chickens. Most of my siblings did. We hated the plucking and cleaning, but the killing—that was different. It was a glory of blood and violence, the chickens clowns for our entertainment. After selecting the plump ones from the flock and nabbing them with a chicken hook—a long, stiff wire that slipped over the animal's leg and held it—we stuffed them into wire cages and carried them to the chopping block, a sawed-off tree stump stained with old blood.

With an ax, wasting little time, Dad methodically laid the chickens' necks on the block and with a single blow chopped their heads off. He threw the bodies aside—and this is what we loved. The chickens flopped around, flapped their wings, leaped with both legs off the ground, as if trying to fly away from what had happened to them.

All we saw was the dance, the antics, and it made us laugh. I can't excuse this or explain it. The chickens seemed like fools, partly. They seemed excited. They seemed crazy, wild, carefree, they seemed to have broken all animal sense of decorum. To children, constricted in their actions, constantly checking the boundaries of emotion and behavior, the sight of something breaking those boundaries is funny. A child has a hard time telling the difference between a madman and a clown, and may laugh at or be frightened by either.

For whatever reason, we leaped and skipped with the chickens as they did their headless dance of death, seeming more vibrant than they ever were when alive. It was so much fun that I wanted to help chop the heads off, to instigate this riot. Dad never let me. No, he would say—just that, without explanation—when I asked.

Then one year he said yes. I was perhaps ten years old, and I asked, as I had for several years, if I could chop a chicken's head off, and this time, instead of his usual no, he handed me the ax. "Just be sure you do it well," he said.

I pulled a chicken out of the cage, held it by its legs, puffed up with pride, sure of myself. I walked to the chopping block, the ax and the chicken hanging from my arms. I swung the bird onto the block. It craned its neck, and I twisted the body to force the head to lie flat on the block.

The chicken's eye looked up at me. It looked up at

me, holding the ax, and I realized what I was about to do—snuff out that bead of awareness, annihilate whatever intelligence and sentience was there. Suddenly I felt accused. I felt guilty. I felt remorse sweep into me. I felt helpless and afraid.

Dad was waiting. All these years I'd asked to do this, and now I had my chance, and I wanted to back out. But I couldn't. He was watching, and I suddenly understood that if I didn't do this, he would have to. I sensed at a wordless level that he had never enjoyed it, had never seen the fun we saw in it, that it was an obligation for him—a have-to, not a want-to. If I didn't go through with it, he would.

What had seemed privilege became responsibility. What had seemed power became helplessness. I forced myself to raise the ax and bring it down below the staring eye—but I didn't do it well. I caught the neck a glancing blow, and the chicken squawked. Blood spurted. Horrified, I raised the ax again and this time caught the neck full-on. I threw the body from me, where it flopped on the grass, but this time I wasn't watching. The eyelid of the chicken's head lying on the block blinked twice, slowly, the eye with each blink losing light and glitter, the comb paling and fading, until lid and comb both were bluish-white.

Never after that could I laugh and skip at chicken-killing time. I didn't protest it, didn't refuse to eat chicken or quit relishing its flavor. I wasn't sickened by what we did. I was simply no longer above or ignorant of death.

Chopping a chicken's head off while its bright eye

looks up at you—surely this seems cruel. How did my father know when the time was right for it? A year earlier or a year later I might have gloried in the power or been unable to make an imaginative connection and realize what I was doing. Why was it all a lesson in gentleness, and how did he know it would be? He never asked me to do it again. He wasn't giving over a responsibility to one of his children. He was only teaching.

I found the baby rabbit, mauled and bloody, by Tippy's dish. Why the dog hadn't just killed it I don't know. He hadn't. The rabbit was alive, a small, struggling thing, with gashes along its side and head, breathing its small breaths, silent. I picked it up. Its blood reddened my hands. I looked around for Dad, knew immediately he was in the fields. That was bad. It brought whatever was going to happen to the rabbit closer to me.

I carried the small thing into the house, limp and warm in my palm. I entered the kitchen where Mom was busy doing dishes after lunch. "Look what I found," I said. "It's a baby rabbit. I found it by Tippy's dish. He must have bitten it."

My mother looked. "It's going to die," she said.

I already knew that. I'd seen enough of animals by then—I was thirteen—to know when one would die. Still, it made me angry at Mom to hear her say it, so quickly, without even considering another possibility, without even taking her hands from the dishwater.

"It might live," I said. "If we take care of it."

"No. You'll have to kill it."

"Me?"

"You found it."

There was no discussion here. There was no attempt at comforting illusion. There was no explanation. Her words were absolutely unadorned. She simply expected me to know the moral reasoning: I had found pain, and because I'd found it I was responsible for it; the rabbit was going to die, and the only good thing I could do, the necessary thing, was to kill it quickly. Had my mother put an arm around my shoulder to comfort me and explain all this, I would have rebelled. I would have then been able to see her as the authority figure forcing me to do what I hated. But she explained nothing; she left me with my own conclusions.

I stalked from the house angry at her, because she hadn't allowed me to be angry. I carried the rabbit outside onto the hot, fly-strewn porch. Immediately flies came to it, and I shooed them furiously away, and hurried down the steps. I didn't know what to do. I thought of hiding the rabbit, or of putting it in the grove to let it die and not telling Mom, but I knew this wasn't between me and her. It was between me and the rabbit.

I went to the toolshed. I saw pipes there, angle iron, blocks of wood, rope. In each thing I saw a killing tool. The rabbit had focused my imagination to see in everything a way to take a life. But each thing I saw was brutal, each imaginative act beyond me: smashing the tiny skull with iron or wood, strangling the thin neck with cord. My mind rebelled at the pictures and sounds it conjured.

What could I do? The rabbit lay painfully bleeding

in my palm. Suddenly I thought of my slingshot. I ran behind the grain bins and placed the rabbit on the log fence there, then raced back into the house and upstairs. I grabbed my slingshot off the shelf where I kept it between two model airplanes and raced back downstairs, past my mother, with her hands still in dishwater, who glanced at me going by but didn't ask questions.

On the gravel drive between the house and toolshed I selected four smooth stones. I ducked into the weeds growing between toolshed and grain bins. The rabbit still breathed, dangling formless over the log. I needed space. The weeds grew too tall. I went back to the toolshed and found an iron bar about three feet long. Still clinging to the slingshot and stones, I wielded the bar in a wide arc, knocking the weeds down, making a clear sight line between me and the rabbit. Finally I stood out on the lawn, fifteen yards away from it. From this distance it was only a small lump of brown fur there on the post. It might have been anything.

The third stone hit it. It made hardly a sound from where I stood. I waited a few minutes, then went to the animal and buried it in the grove.

In all of this, who was I being gentle for, who cruel to, and where does the boundary between the two lie? The most brutal and cruel thing I imagined was to simply walk out of the house and with a single blow, holding the rabbit by its hind legs, smash its skull on the sidewalk. Yet, if cruel, it would also have been the most gentle thing. I couldn't bring myself to that terrible gentleness. I needed space and distance. I let the rabbit linger in its suffering so that I could form a world where

I wouldn't hear stone striking bone. It seems to me
now to be sentimentality, not gentleness—and sentimentality can be cruel.

Walking to work a few years ago I heard a rustling in the
bush and found a wounded pigeon, blue-gray and buff,
looking at me with one bright eye. I know of nothing so
askew, so clearly and simply *wrong* as a wounded bird.
Whether at rest or in flight, birds always look right; perhaps it is this quality that attracts us to them. Some fish
have this look, and certain predators, notably the more
dangerous cats, the tiger, leopard, jaguar. But only birds,
as an entire class of animals (with the possible exception
of the vulture and the ostrich) always look right—their
wings outspread in flight, soaring, or tucked in close to
their bodies, compact as torpedoes. Birds always seem
self-contained, where and how they should be.

But a wounded bird is one of the most wrong things
I know. Other animals can hide wounds. A dog can run
on three legs so skillfully we'll hardly notice it. This is
because a dog is rather sloppy and inelegant—efficient in
many ways, but coarsely tuned, redundant. It is only nature's insistence on symmetry that gives a dog four
rather than three legs. But a bird's need for lightness
makes redundancy and profligacy impossible. When a
bird is wounded, in even the smallest way, it takes on the
look of a wind-opened umbrella or a broken tennis racket, the look of light things wound tight and snapped. If
all of nature were as finely tuned, as elegant and lacking
in redundancy as its birds, our wounding activities upon
this planet would be far more visible and apparent.

I knew the pigeon in the bush was wounded the moment I saw it. It looked splayed, angled, broken, its feathers jagged, its wings hanging. It fled from me, trying to take the air, but its movements, like its body, were broken. I knew what had happened—someone had hit it with a car and hadn't stopped. I wished for an example different from my father's.

I set off after the pigeon. Even a wounded bird can move quickly, and I had to trespass upon three neat lawns, leaping a flower bed, before I caught up to it. It tried to hide in another bush. I pinned it there, picked it up, and quickly this time, took its neck in my hand and spun it in a quick wrist-snap, which I'd also learned from Dad.

I know there are many who would argue that a wounded animal, rather than being killed, should be taken to a veterinarian, that humans have no right to make life and death decisions for other species. Nevertheless, I felt that I'd finally done the right thing in the right way. I don't know whether there is a rule written somewhere in the universe or in the mind of God that speaks to what I should have done with the pigeon. Brutal as wringing a bird's neck may be, and though it leaves me still with doubts and apprehensions, it also seems necessarily gentle.

Of course even moral actions are based on knowledge and ability. In this day and age the knowledge of how to wring a bird's neck is highly specialized. If I'd had to question the proper way to do it or, as with the rabbit, look for a stick or stone, I might have been unable to do the job. Perhaps I would have saved the pigeon's life. More likely I would have prolonged its silent suffering.

I'm left, finally, with no answers other than the mystery of relationship itself. The old adage to stop and smell the roses isn't just about slowing down your life. It's about letting the world enter you, letting yourself come into relationship with it, taking the time to be changed by it. But it's not just roses, and it's not just things that are pleasant. When Dad stopped the car for that wounded bird, he was allowing himself to be affected by it, allowing the course of his life to change.

Human beings can choose such things. Dad might have decided getting to church on time was more important than the bird fluttering into the field. He might have decided to maintain the course he'd planned. When he stopped the car instead, he opened the door to a relationship with the animal—and once you do that, so much becomes ambiguous.

A bit of life, bound in feathers, leaps in a random vector to intersect our speed. We stop, or we go on. We accept the world's sudden offering of relationship or we reject it. Part of the offering is an invitation to cruelty, part an invitation to gentleness. If we can't always tell the difference between the two, still, as human beings, it's best to try. This seems to me the larger lesson of my father's example, of his handing me the ax, and of my mother's expectation that I deal with the rabbit: the world is here; will you notice it, relate to it, be changed by it? Stopping to smell the roses or stopping to catch the bloodied birds and hold them in your hands—the world calls us to be part of it, but doesn't always tell us how.

The
Night Trucks

The cattle trucks came at night so that they would arrive at the stockyards in the morning. Their lights down our long driveway in late winter cut shadows across the upstairs bedroom where my brothers and I slept, the web of the naked elm in the front yard moving slowly over the walls like an ineffective net. Shadows of crooked branches slid over the wall above my bed, over the ceiling, over my sleeping brothers, over the model cars and airplanes we had built and placed on shelves, over the chifforobe where we each had a drawer to store personal things. The gray Formica kitchen table with its wavy patterns of white seemed almost to disappear in the moving shadows. It had come to our room after Dad brought home from an auction sale the great black wooden table that had made Mom cry when she saw it, but which she couldn't refuse because the family had grown too large for the smaller table.

The shadows made the bedroom seem underwater, light coming down through a broken surface, from a distant world. I watched them for a while, then climbed down from the bunk bed and walked through them as they rose over my bare feet from the floor. For a while, before going downstairs, I stood at the window over the porch roof to see the great trucks, framed by their orange running lights, descend the long driveway and pull idling into the yard.

Dressed in coveralls and overshoes, I went out to diesel smoke in the cold air, and throbbing engines, and the drivers' faces in their mirrors as they labored at the wheels, backing around the granary, twisting the trailer so that it eased, with a sigh of air brakes, up to the wooden chute placed at the barn door, through which came the muffled sound of moving animals.

Steam filled the barn. Men and beasts moved obscurely in a white fog lit by dim bulbs, the cold air gusting through the door, heightening the smell of manure. Hooves clattered on the wooden chute. Steers tried to go up two at a time, grunting, snorting, until someone at the chute forced one of them back. The whole barn heaved and roiled. The animals approached the chute head down, legs ready to spring away, until one made the move, and then others followed.

We'd sorted them during the day, gathered them close to the barn and then walked among them, forming judgments. When young, we were just cutters, bringing the ones Dad wanted to see to his inspection, and then, if he decided, chasing them into the barn. The cattle tried to dodge back into the herd and we followed them, singling them out. Even at a young age we could tell one steer or heifer from another, and eventually we'd cut the one Dad sought. He'd look at it, make a decision.

As we got older we learned without formal training, simply by the repetition of finding in the herd the ones he wanted to see, to recognize for ourselves which ones were ready. Then we brought them forward without his orders, and as we got older still we joined the discussion with him, pointing out aspects to a particular steer that made it finished.

We didn't particularly like selling cattle. It was exciting, of course, the dark night, the immense trucks, the contained sense of secrecy and large event in it. But we had walked among these cattle for almost a year, pulled their ears as we paced the bunks, named many of them, learned their idiosyncrasies. There was always a feeling of loss in selling. At the same time we knew it was necessary, like so many other necessary things. The day after the cattle were sold we'd all listen to the morning market reports on WCCO radio to see how well we'd done, to wonder if we could have done better.

And then, always, within a few months, the new calves would arrive, frightened, snorting, scouring, running from the daytime trucks that released them to huddle against the windbreak. And we would feed them. And they would grow used to us. They would grow tame. They would grow fat. Until we would walk among them, judging, dispassionate and critical, and nod our heads, and chase certain of them into the barn.

The year after night came, my brothers and I walked alone among them, having completed the final cycle.

We sold them in batches, as Dad had always done, the finished ones first, then feeding the remaining ones for a few more weeks, sorting again, feeding, the trucks coming down the long driveway, going away, coming. Like so many other things, we discovered that we knew how to do this. We no longer needed Dad to make the final decision. We could look at a steer and tell a finished one from an unfinished. It surprised us. Perhaps it shouldn't have, given how long we'd been doing it; the surprise was in discovering what we hadn't known we knew. It was a small pleasure, and perhaps a foolish one, to discover such competency in a year of such loss.

Then the final truck came. By then the haymow was empty of all but a few bales of hay. The silo was empty. The corncribs had only a few piles left. We had planned it that way. We knew what was needed to finish the final herd.

Hooves boomed in the metal trailer. The trailer rocked and swayed. One by one the last cattle leaked away through their own fog, flesh turned insubstantial as shadow. They disappeared through the cloud of their own warm breath, through the chaos of their own confusion, until the barn stood empty, rags of mist in the rafters, and the sound of a diesel engine shifting through its gears and axles echoed from the county road—a rectangle of orange and red running lights, headlights pointed away. We watched. Listened. Then turned toward the house. Snow creaked under our overshoes. The stars were cold.

Selling
the Parts

Some men arrived early, to look over the machinery and determine its worth. Once they'd checked things out they passed time by going places they had no right to go. Two of them, dressed in overalls and wearing seed-corn caps, wandered away from where the machinery was parked, crossed the yard in front of the house, leaned on the west cattle yard fence, and then drifted to the barn. I saw them from inside the house and thought to tell them there was nothing for sale where they were going. By the time I left the house they were approaching the barn, their backs to me, and I hurried to catch them.

I was close enough to hear their voices when, to my disbelief, they opened the latched barn door and walked inside. I wouldn't have been more surprised if they had walked into the house. Then I heard something that stopped me.

"This is where he had his cattle?" one of them asked, his voice leaking through the permeable walls.

The other one must have nodded.

"Not much to it," the first voice said. "Is there?"

"Sure isn't."

I heard their steps coming to the door and ducked into the narrow space between the silo and the first grain bin, back near the log fence we balanced on when we were kids, trying to see if we could walk the entire length on the logs, which thinned as we progressed, until walking on them was like walking on a spring. They picked up our rhythms, resonated with them, and threw us off, into the weeds on one side or the cattle yard on the other. I went back there, leaned against the logs, and waited for the men to pass.

We are never so vulnerable as when we imagine a privacy that doesn't exist. An auction sale lays your life out for the viewing: these are the things we have used. Anyone can come and look at the hammermill with its bent PTO shaft, the old silage elevator with holes worn through the aluminum, the rope-handled grain baskets, the pitchforks, the silage forks, the hand posthole diggers, the canning jars stacked in dull blue array in cardboard boxes on the back of the splintered bale rack. Anyone at a farm auction can peer at these things, touch them, and make judgments.

A farm auction is a strange invitation of the public into the private sphere. It may seem odd to those who haven't gone through it, but when you lay things out for an auction, you want them to be mere objects. You want them stripped of anything but material value. The old "H" tractor was the one Dad used for planting corn, and when I thought of it I thought of him sitting on its metal seat in his chambray shirt, his eyes tracing emergent green lines in the soil, formed by future points of rising corn. I couldn't afford to sell those memories, or the memories of driving that tractor the year after he died, tracing the lines for him—so I reduced the "H" to metal, to a machine, to whatever *use* it had, in order to keep from losing everything when the auctioneer cried out and pointed to the winning bidder.

We sorted the equipment and made our choices first. Does anyone want the electric drill? The welder? This extension cord? I took a brace and a set of bits, among a few other things, for their sentimental value, because I love hand tools, and because they were so well made, and because of the memories I had of being a child and drilling holes in scrap wood, loving how the shavings curled out of the hole and piled up, full of scent, and how the bit drove downward, screwing itself into the wood.

Other things we turned back to the material world. I allow the brace to carry memory, allow the touch of its handle to return me to the first time Dad showed me how to use it, his hands on it, my hands taking it, my wonder at its magic, the smell of fresh pine shavings mingling with the smell of old oil in the toolshed. When I let my own children use it, their never-known grandfather is passing it to them, his presence is given them, they touch the past, touch where and who they've come from.

Such things were chosen carefully. The flip side of

sentiment is practicality, and the vast majority of things we divested of memory and meaning, reduced them to their material worth. The "H" tractor was an "H" tractor, not Dad's life. We lined it up and waited for bidders.

It would be easy to be cynical about auction sales, to see them as vulture feedings, everyone come to get a deal out of death. That is certainly one of the reasons people come, but it's justifiable. What are the living to do with death but deal with it, and get a deal from it if they can? In any case, if there is at some funerals a sense of bargain making, of agreeing through the barter of words to ensure the safe passage of a soul or to value a life in a way it was never valued while lived, there is also at auction sales a sense of religious ritual. The chant of the auctioneer, the grunts of the spotters calling the bids, have a revivalist quality, like preaching and amens. And like attending funerals, people attend auction sales partly out of obligation and as a form of support, the recognition of community.

Strangers may come merely to buy, but neighbors come to bid. The two things are very different. The word *auction* comes from a Latin word meaning "to increase," and bidding is the way this increase is accomplished. The stranger's victory at an auction sale is to buy something cheaply. The neighbor's victory is to run a bid up, to risk going beyond what something is worth, thus transferring more wealth to the coffers of the bereaved.

For the family, an auction sale brings a feeling of both anticipation and helplessness. We were not merely offering something for sale at a price, take it or leave it.

We were offering everything for sale, for whatever the auctioneers could get for it. Even having done the emotional preparation, having consigned things back to the material world, it was not easy to watch a way of life go, to see things we had handled and worked with, things Dad's hands had worn smooth—to see these things given up for nothing more than what someone else, with a nod of the head, decided they were worth.

Of course ways of life go whether you watch or not. By the time the auction occurred I had been accepted into college, not intending to return to farming. I was leaving in an ordinary way, for the promise of a future, not because of the loss of a past. Still, an auction sale is like a certification of loss, a stamp of certainty. Nothing makes a decision more clear and solid than to see someone you don't know climb onto the seat of a tractor you've driven since you were ten and start it up and put it in gear and, once on the driveway, open the throttle so that the tractor emits its familiar roar, pours a single cloud of blue smoke out its exhaust, and follows the diminishing perspective of the driveway up to the county road, its roar thinning as its outline does, until tractor and stranger are gone altogether, together. After everything is gone, emptiness is left. Space. When you walk in it, you hear your life echoing.

Still, all this was bearable. It was, after all, what we planned for, talked about, and expected. What I hadn't expected was the rupture of the private sphere by strangers, so much different than the careful reserve and precise timing of the neighbors who came to combine our corn the previous fall, breaking into our private

sphere as well, but as an invitation to, and acknowledgment of, community, not as simple carelessness or
voyeurism.

Most people who come to an auction realize that,
though the sale is open to the public, it is held on private
land and is for the family a private happening. Those
who realize this confine themselves to the area demarcated as public by the presence of things for sale. None
of this is spoken or signed, nothing roped off. Everything depends on custom and courtesy. There are always
rogues, though, who understand nothing *but* directions, or whose curiosity is greater than their sensibility.

The west barn *wasn't* much. It was old, it was sagging,
it had holes in the cedar shingles. It was an old dairy
barn, with stanchions for milking cattle and cement
troughs to collect urine and manure. Before I was born,
Dad switched from dairy to beef cattle. The stanchions
became useless, and the gutters, no longer cleaned
every day, filled with straw and manure. Several times a
year we had to clean the entire barn out with pitchforks,
one of our least favorite jobs.

Above the barn was a haymow, or loft. The roof of
the barn sloped down on the west side and we stacked
straw there, cramming the bales into the slope, leaving
the large main space for hay. When I was young I loved
riding on the full hayracks. They shifted and groaned as
Dad pulled them in from the fields. They felt like they'd
fall over, especially when he went up the slope of the
road ditch, the bales moving under me like an animal
swaying.

He pulled them up to the elevator we'd placed in

the haymow door. Usually one of us unloaded the rack, while two helped Dad in the haymow. Unloading was considered the better job: there was air. Baling took place in June, July, and August. By the time the sun had dried the dew from the hay, it had also turned the hay-mow into an oven. The bales came up the elevator and we pulled them off the side, gripping the twine with gloved hands, and carried them, in the stifling heat, to the stack. Back and forth, one by one, the elevator screeching, we hauled hundreds of bales of hay, each weighing about sixty pounds, and stacked them on top of each other until the stack reached the ceiling of the haymow and there was only a narrow crawl space in the apex of the roof. Over the years the weight drove the pillars supporting the loft right through the concrete in the barn below, so that the concrete buckled and rose.

Evening after evening through the year we emptied the haymow, throwing out five or six bales of hay a day to feed the cattle. As the loft emptied, its topography changed; we found tunnels between the stacked hay and the slope of the roof, played hide-and-seek in them, invented games to play on the towering cliffs stepping down to the floor. When we got older Dad bought a basketball hoop and net and erected it in the front of the barn when the hay had been cleared away enough to form a small court. As winter progressed the court grew in size. We played after chores, in weather cold enough to see breath, the single lightbulb up in the ceiling barely illuminating the rim in the dusty air.

On that court we were hard to beat. When we played cousins or friends who were taller or more skilled, the court evened things out. We knew every loose board that would send the ball skewing away from the dribble or trip you when you thought you had a clear drive to the basket. We knew how to shoot at the slightly bent hoop and how to power the ball up hard on a layup, since the board behind the hoop was loose and absorbed the shot. We knew where the holes in the floor were and how to step around them. A visiting cousin, seeking position for a pass, once simply disappeared through the hole that the ladder to the loft came through. Since his teammate in possession of the ball didn't see him go for the pass and since our defense was chaotic rather than strict man-to-man, no one particularly missed him. It was five minutes and several baskets before we noticed his absence and found him crumpled on the floor of the barn below with a severe concussion.

The day Dad had his stroke and Mom had taken him to the hospital, all four of my brothers and I, after we'd finished afternoon chores, went to the nearly empty haymow and played basketball. We had no idea what was going on, no idea what the future would bring, and no language, even, to talk about it. Dad was gone. Mom was with him. Time was here to be filled. It was a Sunday. Once we'd done the necessary work, we looked around and felt the vastness.

It was a strange thing, in many ways. Something terrible had just happened. Everything had changed, we weren't sure how. And we went to the haymow, by mutual need and desire, and had a great game of basketball, laughing and grunting, throwing up the dust, spinning and ducking over the loose boards, passing to each other, calling to each other, the barn swallows that nested in the ceiling flying in and out through the broken windows, the new kittens in their nests of straw in the back mewing in the absence of their mother.

We had fun. We had great fun. We spoke a little about what had happened, expressed a few doubts and fears. The game allowed that, but was always there to break us from those fears when they got too dark. We weren't in denial. We were together. Our cries for a pass, our shouts of encouragement, echoed in a space that had formed our lives. It was the beginning of a new way of dealing with the world, where we were going to have to stick together. Dad was deathly ill—but that basketball game was one of the best times I ever had with my brothers, and that's no paradox at all.

After Dad died the haymow remained empty. We didn't fill it that summer, knowing we would feed the cattle out. Instead we planted all cash crops that spring, and the basketball net stayed up, no need to take it down.

So it was up when those two strangers, breaking all common courtesy and respect, boldly walked into the barn and made their foolish, material observations: "It isn't much." They didn't see the basketball hoop, of course. They saw the concrete cracked underneath the pillars. They saw the holes in the walls. And if they had seen the basketball hoop, their observation would have been the same: not much. It was a cheap basketball hoop that we'd welded together more than once, with a torn and ragged net. And the floor! My god! You call that a basketball floor?

It would take someone with astounding prescience to see how that was the best basketball floor in the world. If you guarded your man just a bit to the left as he came up the middle, he'd bounce the ball onto that crooked floorboard and it'd leap away from his hands right into yours, an easy steal. No cheating—just knowing the conditions.

It would take someone with even more astounding prescience to read the story of filling and emptying in the hayloft, of work and games, of the way my brothers and I grappled with fear and love in the glory of that game on Palm Sunday when Dad wandered away from his welding. But only people with astounding prescience should leave the parked machinery.

Had the barn been for sale I would have divested it of meaning, done the necessary things to consign it back to the material world from which it had at one time sprung—new, and empty of stories or history, of anything nonmaterial but hope. I would have made the necessary jokes, preempted them in their statements: "That barn won't bring much, full of holes like it is— unless maybe an NBA team would buy it for an arena." Then, seeing the men go into it, I would have been calm, having made the barn safely public, and invited them to look. Hearing their comments I would have chuckled: so predictable.

I hadn't removed memory or meaning from the barn when those men, uninvited, entered it. When they invaded my private and storied life, I didn't know how to confront them. I hid. I went back to the log fence behind the grain bins and stood among the weeds, suddenly ashamed to face those men, to have them look at me and know me as the son of the owner of such a poor barn. The richness still resided there—and that was the problem. I had no idea how to tell those men that, and they had no right to know.

But neither did I know how to tell myself I shouldn't be ashamed. I leaned on the log fence, off-balance, vulnerable, my heart in my throat, this place no longer quite mine, usurped by these strangers, and waited for the men to pass, so that I wouldn't see their faces, so that they wouldn't see mine.

Going Back

The driveway slopes slightly—not enough to notice in a car, but when I was a child on a bicycle I worked up wonderful speed going down it to home, pebbles kicking out from the wheels like sparks, the wind a gale in my face. I stand at the end of the driveway now—no longer a child, the driveway no longer mine—and look down at the old house, a quarter of a mile away. I used to walk this driveway every morning and afternoon to catch the school bus, and often at night I would walk it just to be away, to hear crickets, to kick stones, to lie down in road-ditch grass, to feel night winds.

The driveway was long in those days. Walking to its end guaranteed solitude, especially at night. It was a break from the constant presence of family, a place for private thoughts. If I walked on, cars on the county road might intrude with headlights and dust, but on

the driveway silence was a sturdy thing, darkness complete, and distance adequate.

Standing just in from the road now, I look at the
house, barely visible behind the spreading trees. I never
realized how private the place appeared from the
road—like a retreat and a haven. But the elms have
spread a great deal since we left, and the maples have
grown from spindly sticks to full-fledged trees that
reach the roof peak. I start down the driveway, the sun
hot. It's been a four-mile run from my mother's house
in town. My wife and children are there now, in air-
conditioned rooms, but I've taken this notion to run
out here, and now I'm questioning the wisdom of it.
Still, I have all day. I can walk back if I have to. And it's
only a quarter mile more to the green shade of those
trees, and relief from the standing sun.

I go slowly, resting. The grass, I note, still creeps
onto the driveway, encroaching, a patient growth. Cut
down by mowers, by cars, by the clumsy, ancient road
grader we pulled behind the Oliver, it still comes back.
It will outlast them all, a green persistence. Even without a bicycle I feel the slope in my legs, pulling me easily
down to the small hollow of the buildings, the gravel
scraping and squirting beneath my running shoes. The
telephone poles roll quickly by me, seven of them,
drooping wire.

I stop running as I near the buildings. The new
owners' dog stands near the house, legs spread, and
barks at me. I've called ahead and said I might come
out, and was told the dog wouldn't bite.

The chicken brooder house, which sat alongside the

driveway in front of the garden, is gone. That doesn't surprise me much. It was only half-standing when Mom moved to town, blown over by a strong wind so that it rested on its side. We managed to right it, but it was always shaky after that, leaning toward the ground.

But the apple orchard! Of seven trees, only two remain, small and gaunt among long grass. The apples from this orchard were the surest taste of summer I knew. They never had worms. The growing pullets ate all the moth larvae, running thick-hipped beneath the trees, roosting at night in the branches until Dad sent us out with sticks and flashlights to poke them out and carry them back to the brooder house. Already stupid, chickens were even stupider in the dark. They fell out of the trees like sacks and huddled on the ground until we picked them up.

When the time came to move all those pullets to the henhouse, where they could begin laying eggs to pay us for the water and feed we had carried all summer, we had to catch them and put them into crates and haul them in the pickup to the other side of the farmstead. There were always a few hardy ones that had taken up residence in the grove, following some trickling of instinct for green and shady places. They crossed the cattle yard, found the trees, and stayed there.

The only way to catch them was the same way we caught the ones that roosted in the apple trees—wait until dark and then wander through the grove with flashlights, searching the trees for white lumps while mosquitoes buzzed in our ears. When our lights revealed their pale white bodies, we took long poles and thrust half-blind at them until they tumbled out of their high, safe places. We pounced on them and held them by one leg, upside down, three and four in a hand, and carried them to their more domestic cousins in the henhouse.

In time we learned that, though the chickens could initially outrun us, half-flying, our stamina gave us the upper hand. After that we simply ran them down during the day, making sneak attacks on the grove, turning it into another game we played there, blasting through the burdock and burning weed while the chickens, legs tucked, tried to soar above it but soon wore out and collapsed back into the greenery, where we found them, so tired they ran in dizzy little circles, clucking helplessly. Turning the job of catching chickens into even more of a game, I made a light Argentine bola, of the sort the gauchos use to catch cattle and the giant flightless rhea, and I whirled this above my head and sent it sailing at the chickens. I never caught one with it, though I wrapped it around power poles and fence posts often enough to know that it worked, if only I could throw it accurately.

There are, of course, no chickens now. The people who live here aren't farmers. They work in town. I've slowed to a walk. The dog quits barking, sits on its haunches, and watches me. The farmstead appears strangely as it did when we left, except that everything is empty. No cattle stand at the waterers, staring, their blunt heads motionless. Light comes through the slats of the corncribs. The cement of the cattle yard is clean, the feed bunks gone. The east barn has a dry smell, an old smell. This is where we found a muskrat once, so far from water, and we ran from it, fearing rabies. In this alley between the barn and granary, where Dad sprinkled the Golden Malrin, a "city cousin," excited about driving a tractor, ran over Joel's leg. And just around the corner of the barn the same cousin talked his younger brother into touching the electric fence. We couldn't imagine how anyone could be so ignorant as to willingly touch an electric fence.

I walk on, cooling in the shade of the grove near the corncrib where the steer almost ran me over. The iron pile, which I raided for old leaf springs to make steel crossbows, is almost buried in weeds. From this iron pile, I also fashioned a chicken plucker from a steel drum, an old electric motor, and rubber fingers cut from discarded car tires. We had high hopes for that chicken plucker, thinking it would be our salvation from one of our least desirable tasks. The entire family, including Mom and Dad, came out to watch its debut. I soaked a chicken in boiling water to loosen the feathers, plugged the motor in, and got the rubber fingers spinning. Then I pushed the chicken into them.

Feathers flew everywhere, and for just a moment we all thought a victory had been won over work—until we realized that not only feathers but also skin and meat were flying everywhere. My plucker turned out to be a flayer, and though I tried softening the fingers and slowing down the drum with a larger pulley, I finally gave up, dashing my hopes and the hopes of my siblings.

Within the grove the weeds have grown higher and thicker than ever. We used to keep them down a little just by trampling through them, but now the burning weeds are thick and dark, impassable and severe. They hide the woodpile, where we often came with hammers and nails and saws to spend the afternoons making houses or barns or paddlewheel boats propelled by rubber bands, which we raced in the cattle watering tanks. Dad was always searching for tools that we'd carted to the woodpile and left lying there.

Near the woodpile is the dump rake, obsolete already when we were growing up. Brown with rust, it stands just inside the trees, its curved and pointed teeth looking like some medieval instrument of torture. To turn out hay into windrows for baling we used the newer side rake, but the grass in the road ditches was always a problem. One summer Dad decided to pull the dump rake out of the grove and try it. From then on, to rake hay in the road ditches one of us would sit on the iron seat of the dump rake and another would drive the tractor down the middle of the sloping ditch at what seemed a perilous and imminent angle, ever on the verge of tipping tractor and rake and riders into a curved and pointed catastrophe. But it was really quite safe, and I sang at the top of my lungs once I got used to it, trying to hear myself above the noise of the tractor, while behind me the rake brushed the ground, gathering the loose hay gently, like a comb of steel, into its concave teeth until my brother kicked the lock and the turning wheels raised the teeth into the air, leaving a windrow of hay that we later picked up with pitchforks and fed, unbaled, to the cattle.

The swing set still stands. I can barely remember Dad making it. He wanted his children to have a swing set, but everything in the stores and catalogs looked

small and cheap to him, so he spent several days design-
ing and constructing an immense swing set, welding it
together out of metal pipe, and setting it up between
the old apple trees north of the house, where Mom
could see it easily from the kitchen. Beneath it, in the
shade of the apple trees, we had a huge sandpile. Sandpile and apple trees are both gone now. Dad's swing set,
meant to endure, endures alone, hot to the touch.

The chicken house looks as it always did. The feed
shed next to it—where we locked cats for the night to
catch the mice that grew fat on the grain—still stands,
one of its doors half open, empty now, and no cats waiting to get in.

I've come halfway in my circuit of the buildings. I
turn and start south, back toward the driveway, circling
the house. I won't go into the house. Other people live
there now; I'd feel, I think, a stranger in a place I know
too well.

I walk past the fuel tanks. When Dad wasn't watching we'd sometimes drip a line of gasoline on the
ground and light a match and drop it, watching the
flame race along the ground—small entertainment
while we were filling a thirty-gallon tractor tank. The
box elder tree beside the fuel tanks survives. It always
seemed to be dying, and now, years later, it seems to be
dying still, unchanged.

Behind it, beyond the cattle yard gate, against the
back of the grain bins, is the log fence we balanced on,
where I hid for a while before our auction sale. Weeds
have overwhelmed the cattle yard. Without the constant trampling of hundreds of hooves, the weeds have

taken the opportunity of the manure-rich soil to pour out of the grove. They form a solid mass of head-high green. My father would be shocked. I'm shocked. Yet there's something comforting about their power and insistency, how they won't distinguish between the domestic and the wild, but grow where they're allowed.

I walk past the toolshed, already so full of holes when we left the farm that it couldn't get worse, and it hasn't. The only difference is that it's empty. It used to be crammed with posthole diggers and axes and crowbars and spades, a pick-up-stix tangle of heavy metal and wood, along with the welder and welding supplies, an air compressor and hoses, a cabinet containing files, rasps, electric drills, brace and bits, bolts, screws, and rivets, barrels of hydraulic fluid and engine oil, hydraulic hoses coiled like snakes, belting, swather canvases, and a workbench with a vise. Among all of this there were old harnesses with decorative brass knobs, tarnished with age, that might have been polished and valued as antiques, but that we saw instead, in our practical way, as resources to be cut up if a length of leather was needed.

Dad never painted the toolshed. I think he thought it wasn't worth it. And painting it would have been for him to give up hope that some day there would be enough money to afford the luxury of a new, airtight shop. Perhaps in time there would have been. It stands unpainted now as it always did, its cedar shingles gray.

I walk past the grain bins to the silo—so much time spent up there. I remember the single time Kevin and I got out of sync in our forking and I stepped in front of the door at the moment he swung a forkful of silage at it. The tine went into my calf to the bone. It hardly hurt, and for a while I considered just finishing chores, but then the throbbing started.

I step through the door of the west barn, the one that wasn't "much." It's even less now. The door is half hanging off its hinges. The ceiling is lower than I remember, the air drier, mustier, without the rich, sweet smell of cattle and straw. No baby kittens mew inside the walls.

I climb the ladder to the haymow. It hasn't changed, except that the basketball hoop is gone. A few piles of old hay remain—not worth cleaning out. Light runs in lines through the dusty air, through holes in the shingles. The place echoes with my footsteps. Loose boards clatter underfoot. Sparrows have built a large and dirty nest near the rafters. The floor is littered white.

I go back down, into the sun, and look around. The nape of my neck burns. A barn swallow swoops, glides, disappears through a broken pane into the barn. They still build nests inside then, tight, compact things against the roof. Such cheery birds, strung like beads on the telephone wires, filling the summer air with their graceful flight.

I should spend more time here, I think. But what else is there to do? When I decided to run out here, I thought of the place as full, thought of it as containing hours of memories. But the memories come in a moment, and the place itself is empty. There is the big corncrib that we used to climb, using the slats like a ladder, until we reached the small door onto the catwalk. There we lay when we expected company, watching for the trail of dust above the corn that would signal their arrival. But I'm too old to be climbing corncribs, and I expect no company. Quite the contrary; I am the company.

I look around, trying to feel the place, trying to feel whatever it is I'm feeling, or ought to be feeling. Whatever it is.

I should spend more time here.

I think it again, but walk slowly back toward the driveway. The dog gets up off the porch and barks, to take credit for my departure. This dog has claimed the place. I don't begrudge it that. Still, I wonder: am I so total a stranger? Is there not something of my scent that this animal knows, some faint but deep familiarity caught up from the soil? Does it puzzle, perhaps, in its dim, red brain, over some lost memory of a scent right now urging itself into whatever consciousness a dog might have?

Or not? Is it possible that all those years I spent treading this spot of land, working it, sweating on it, dripping blood upon it time and time again from some cut, some gash, some rip delivered by tool or tin or machine or fall—is it possible that all those years have washed away, that sweat and blood have grown into greenness until not even this dog detects the faintest presence of my molecules clinging in the soil or wood?

I look up at the trees, the elms and maples that have grown so large, and think: It's possible. The place may be in me far more than I in it. We'd like the earth to regret our passing, but we have no proof that it does. I walk past the remains of the apple orchard and start up the slope of the driveway, feeling my legs tighten, becoming hard and stiff. It could be a long run back to town.

The barking recedes, then stops. I am walking slowly, but before I realize it I'm at the end of the driveway, seven telephone poles away from all that I came to see. It's quiet. It's very quiet and very private here at the end of the driveway. I'm alone with my thoughts. Once more I look back. The trees, how they've grown. From here, it all seems a distant, shaded retreat. For a moment I stand still, in the glare of the sun. Then I turn and, on the road, begin to run.

Kent Meyers grew up on a small farm in southern Minnesota, near Morgan, and attended college at the University of Minnesota, Morris, and Washington State University. He currently teaches at Black Hills State University in Spearfish, South Dakota, where he lives with his wife and three children. He has published fiction and nonfiction in literary journals and has won numerous awards for his writing, including the *Minnesota Monthly*'s Tamarack Award and awards from *Crazyhorse*, the *Black Warrior Review*, and the *Southern Humanities Review*.